Picture book of

LANDSCAPES

Breathtaking scenery and beautiful landscapes of nature.

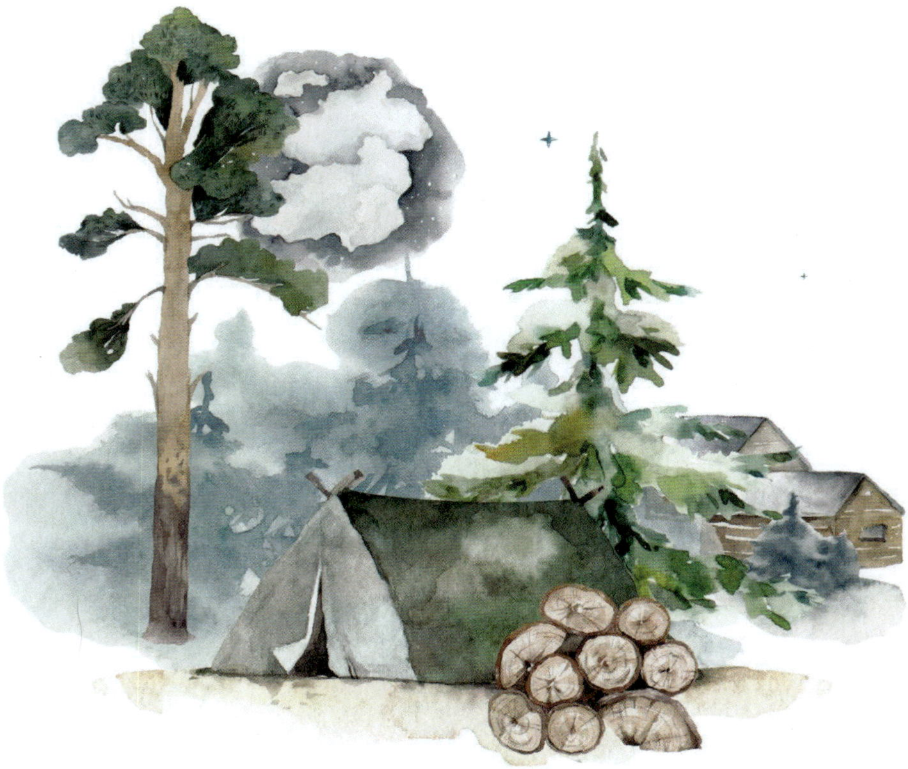

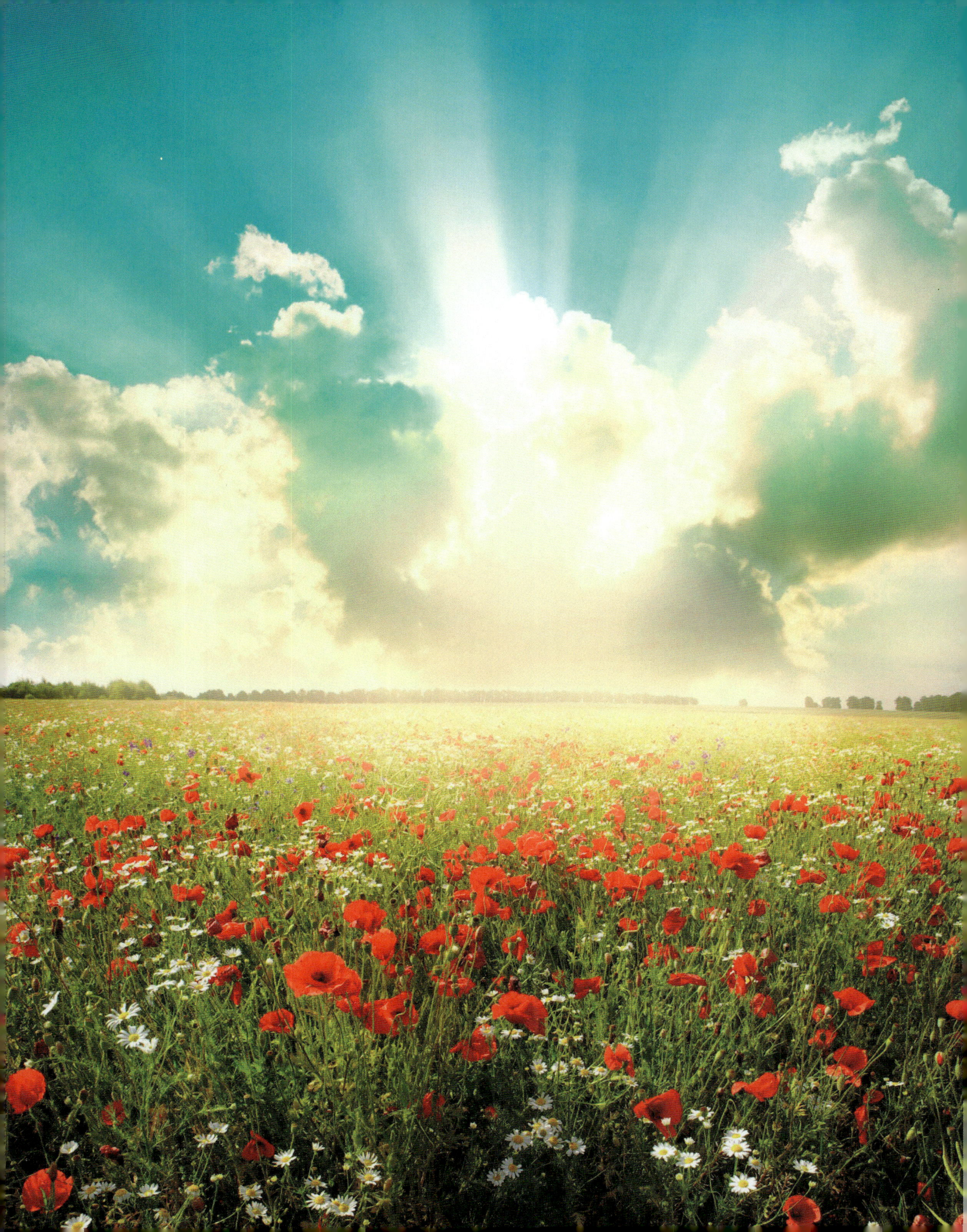

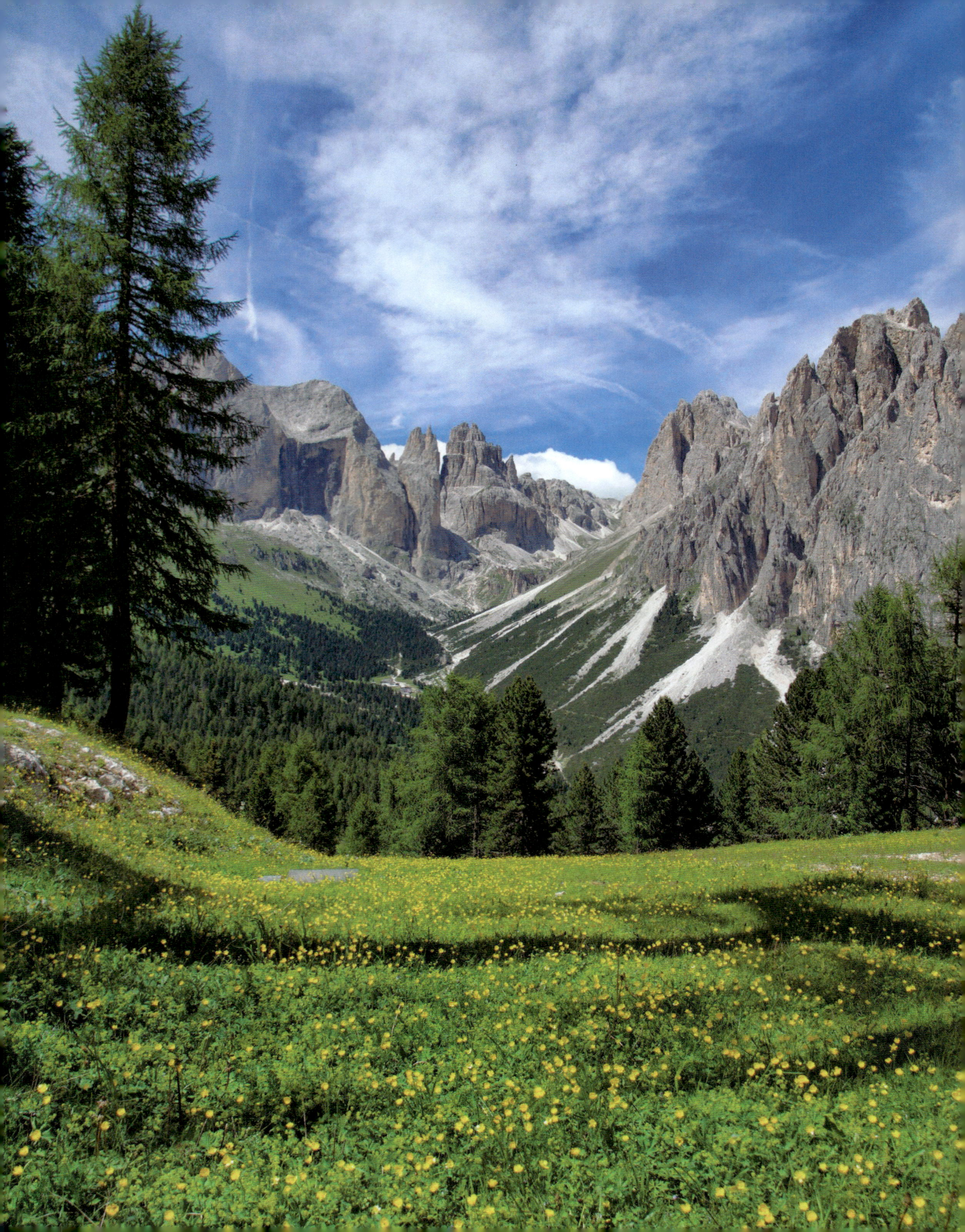

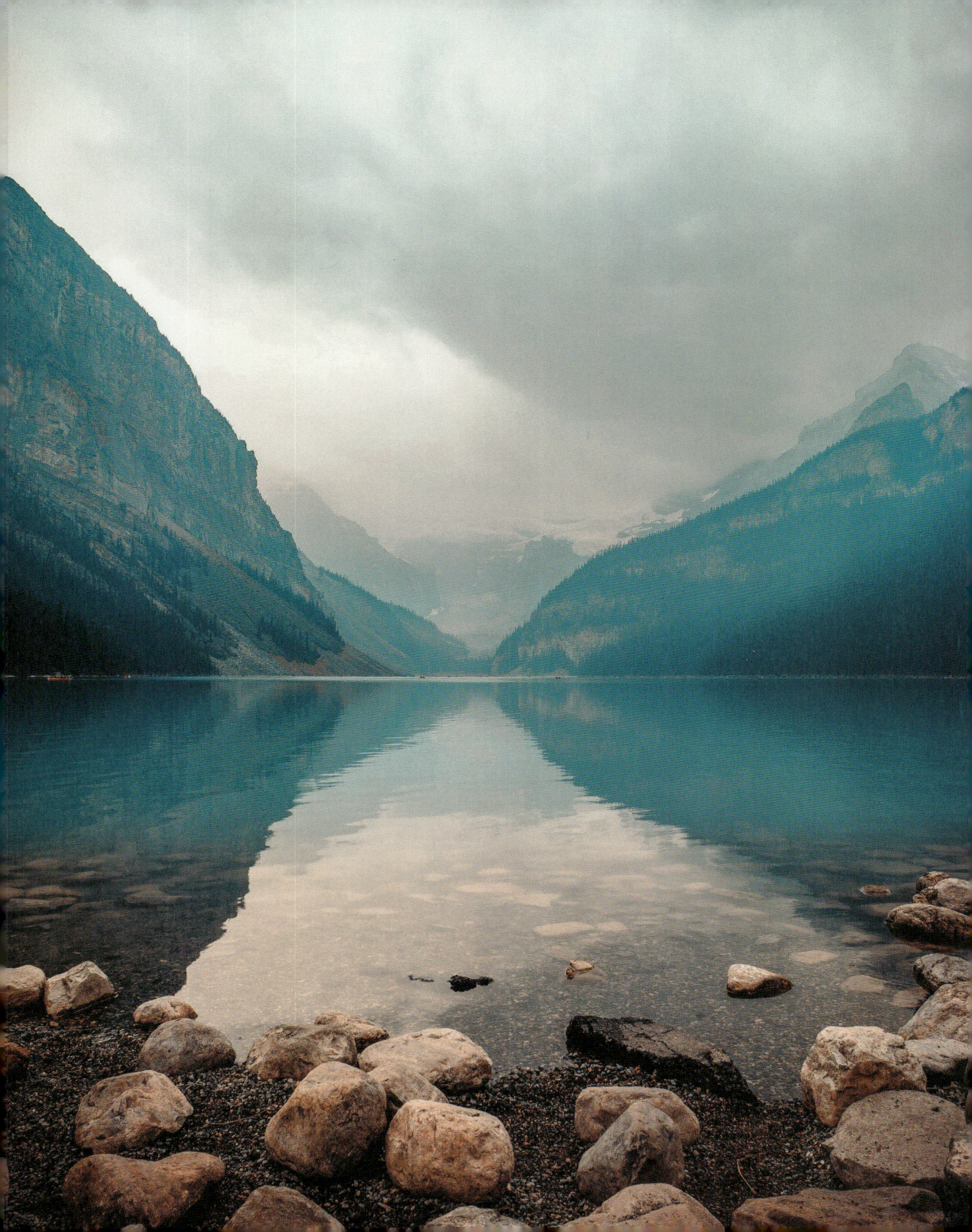

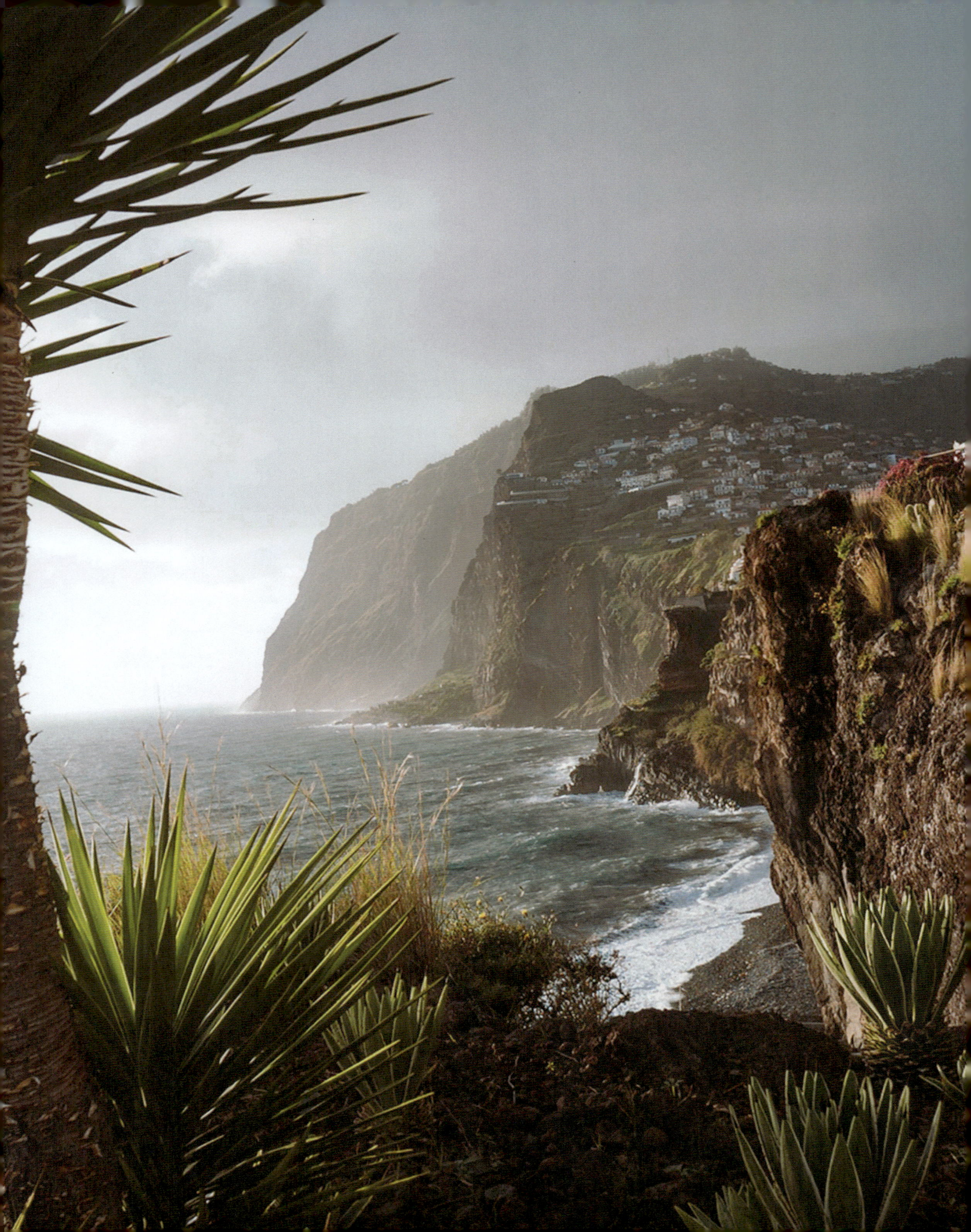

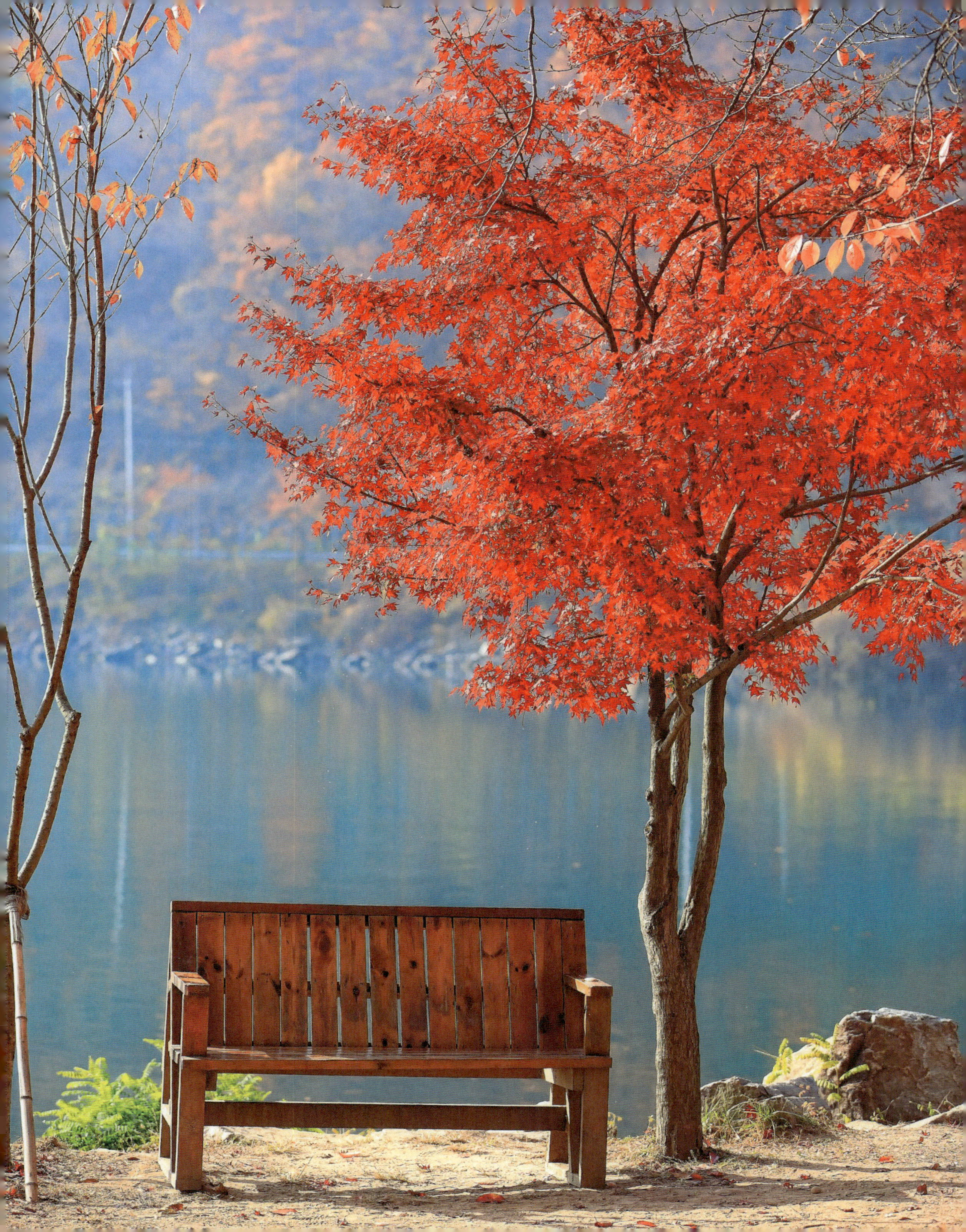

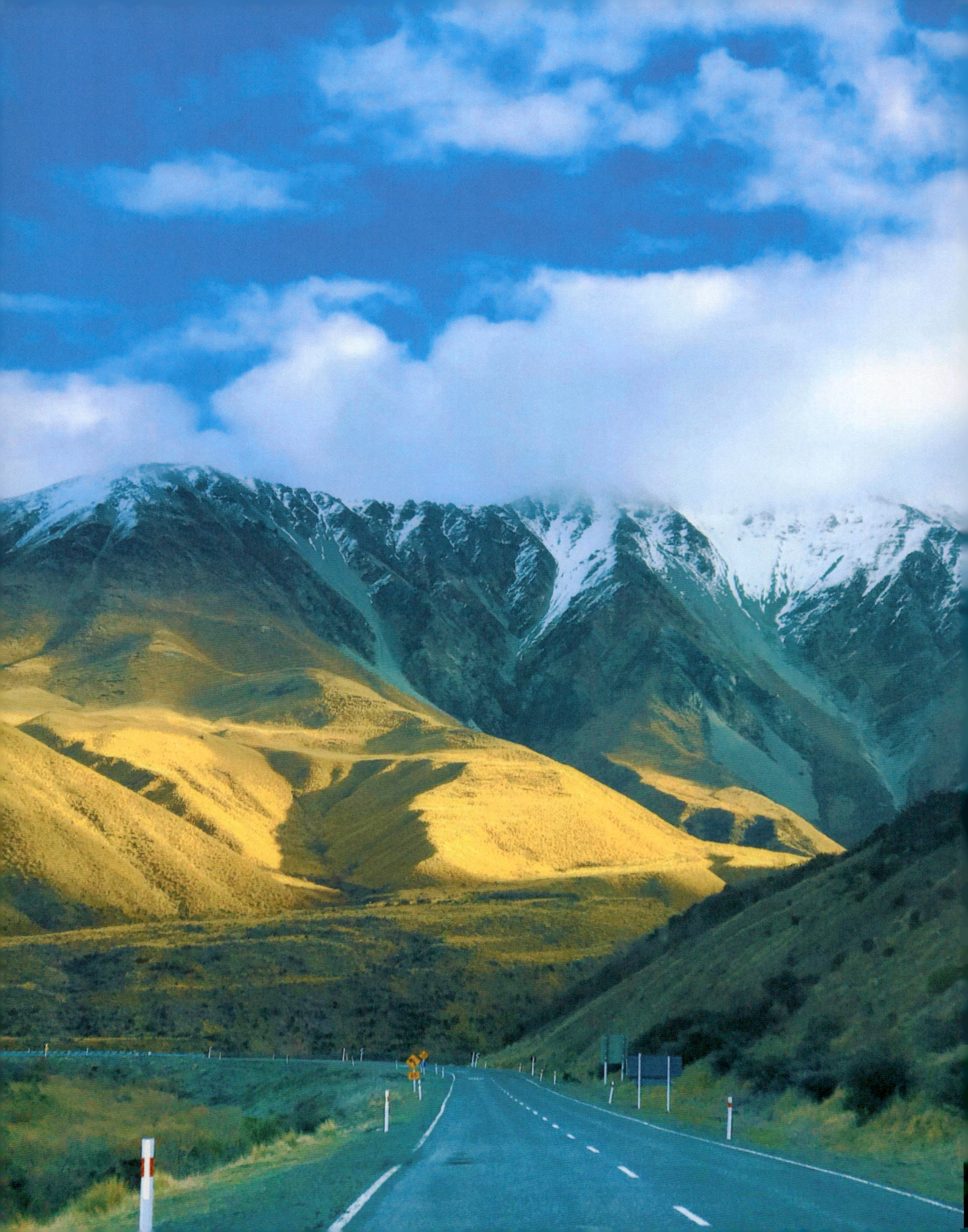

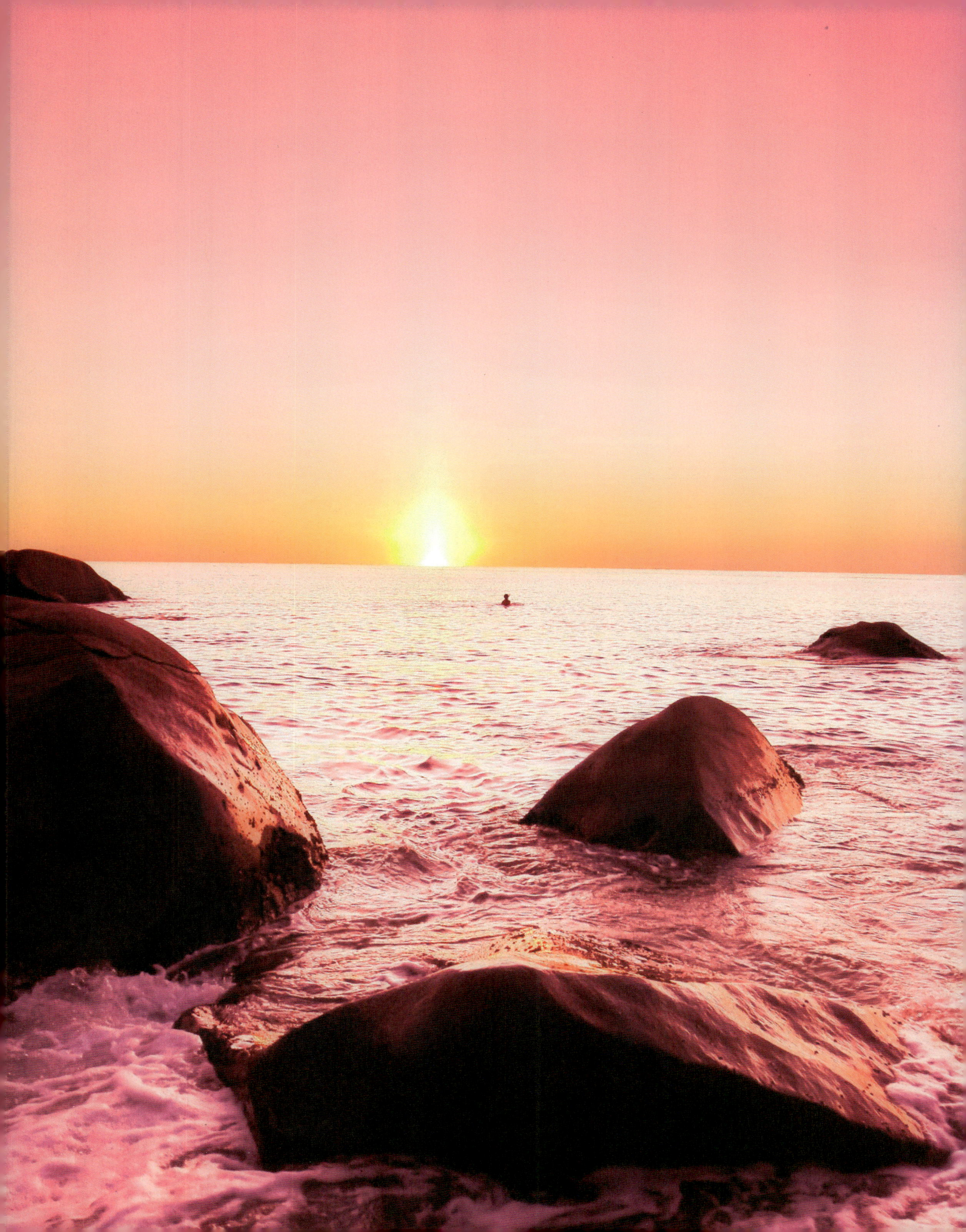

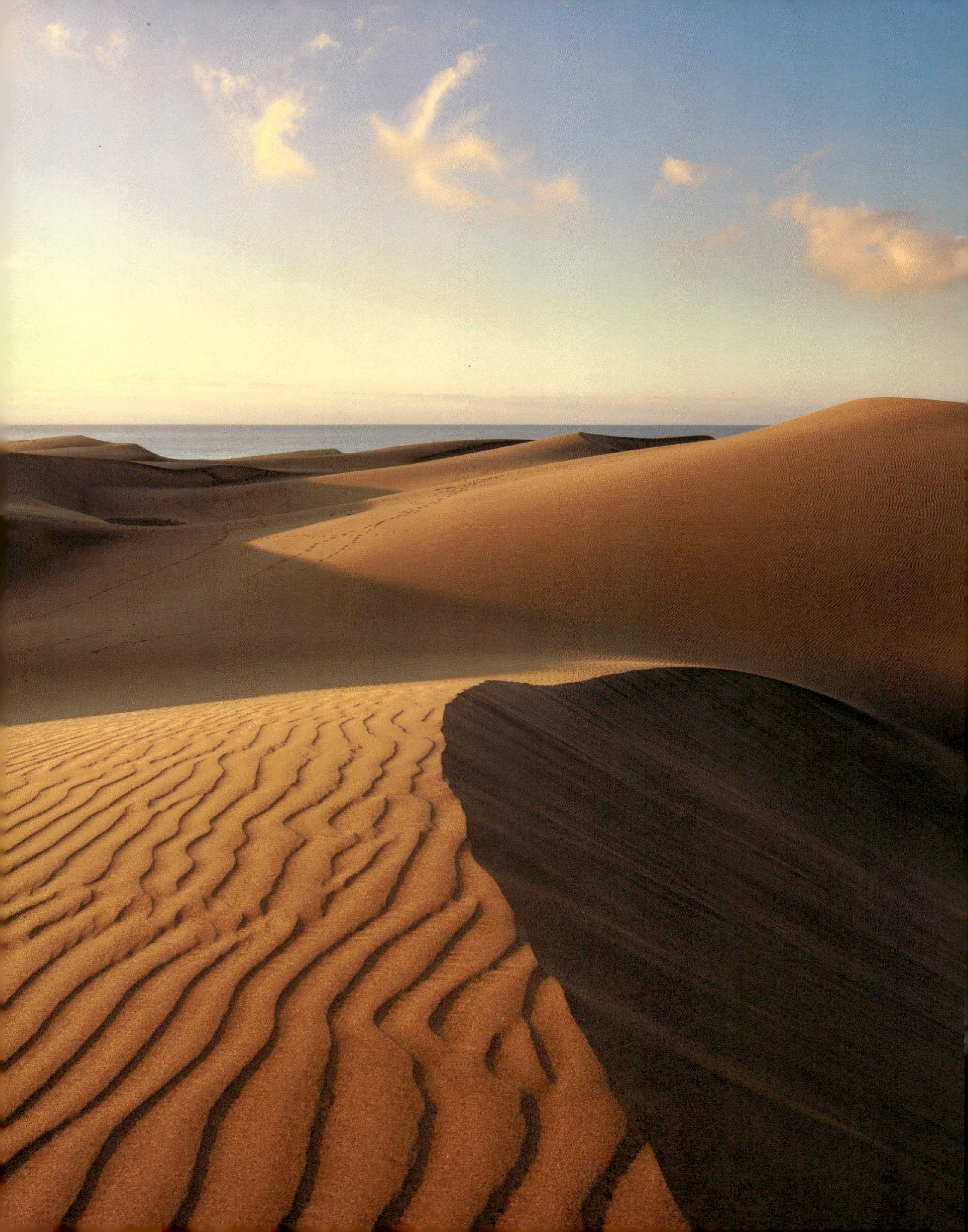

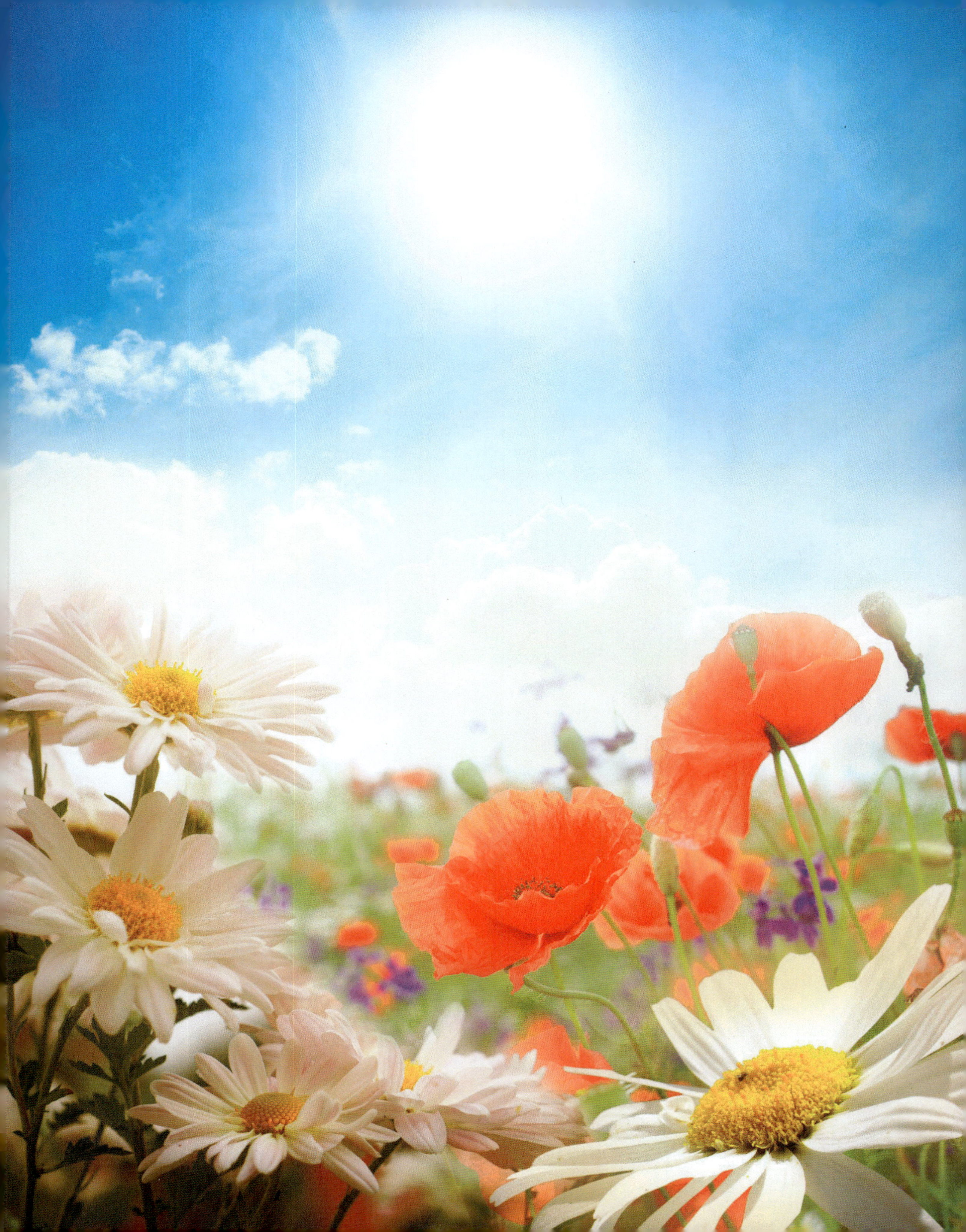

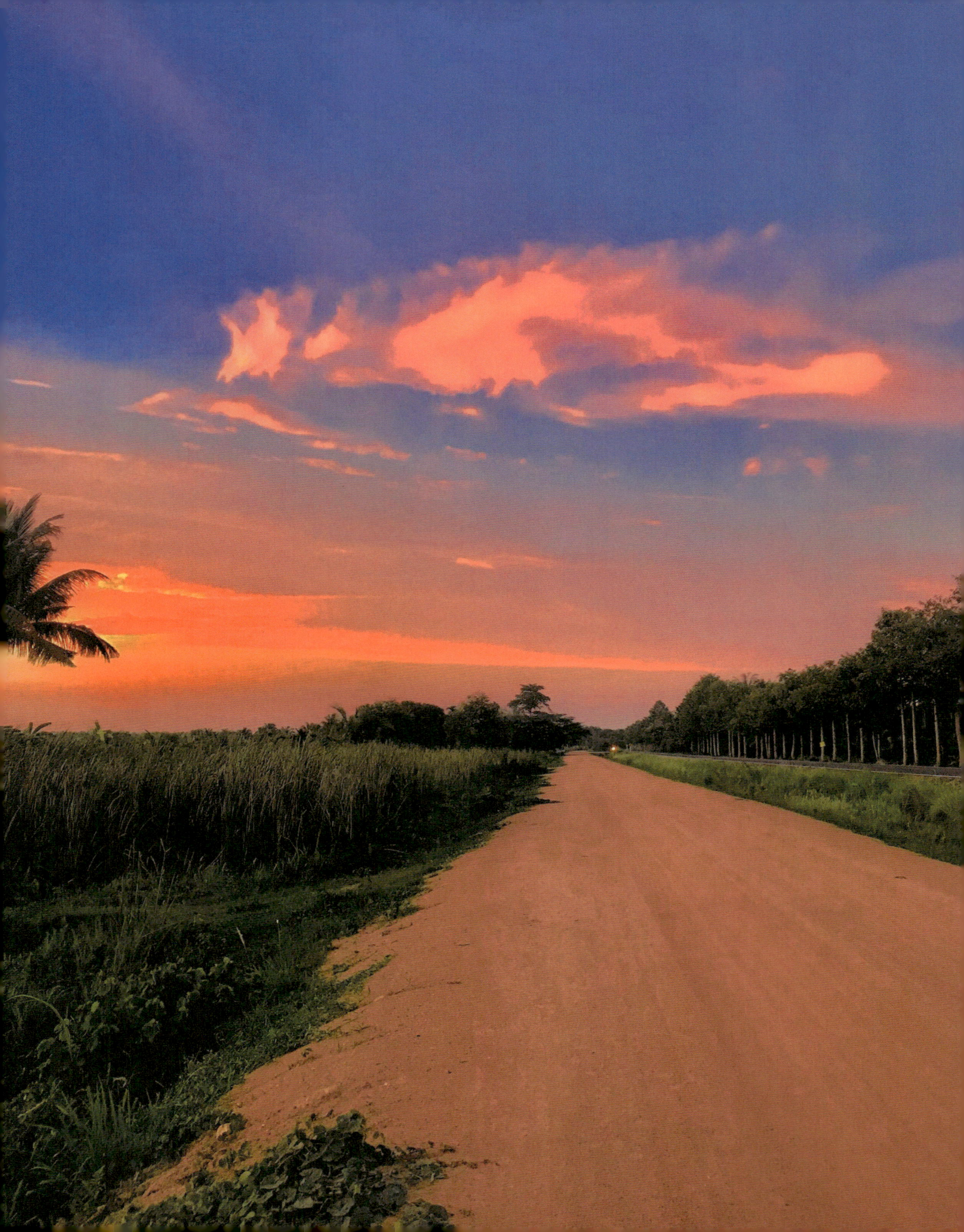

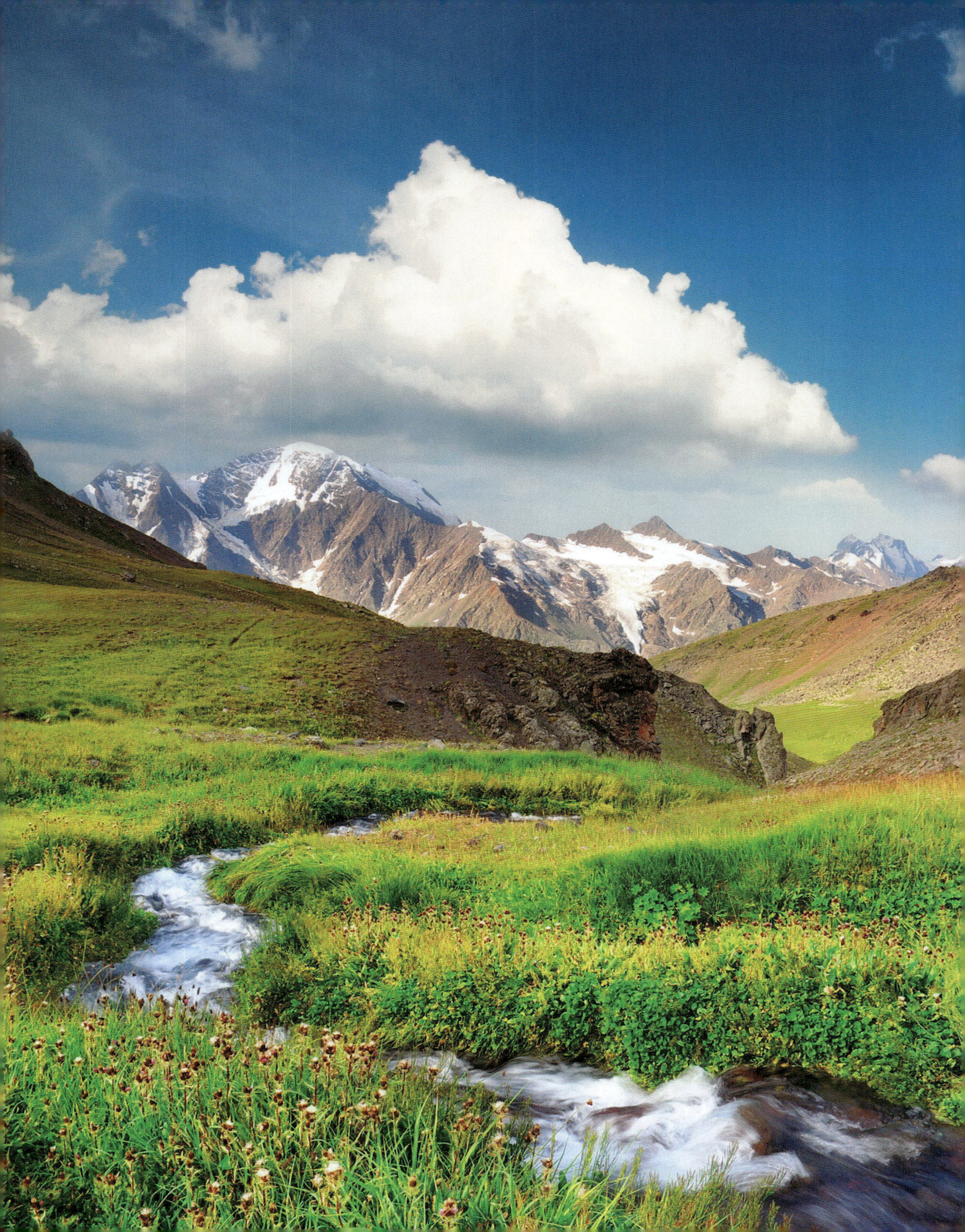

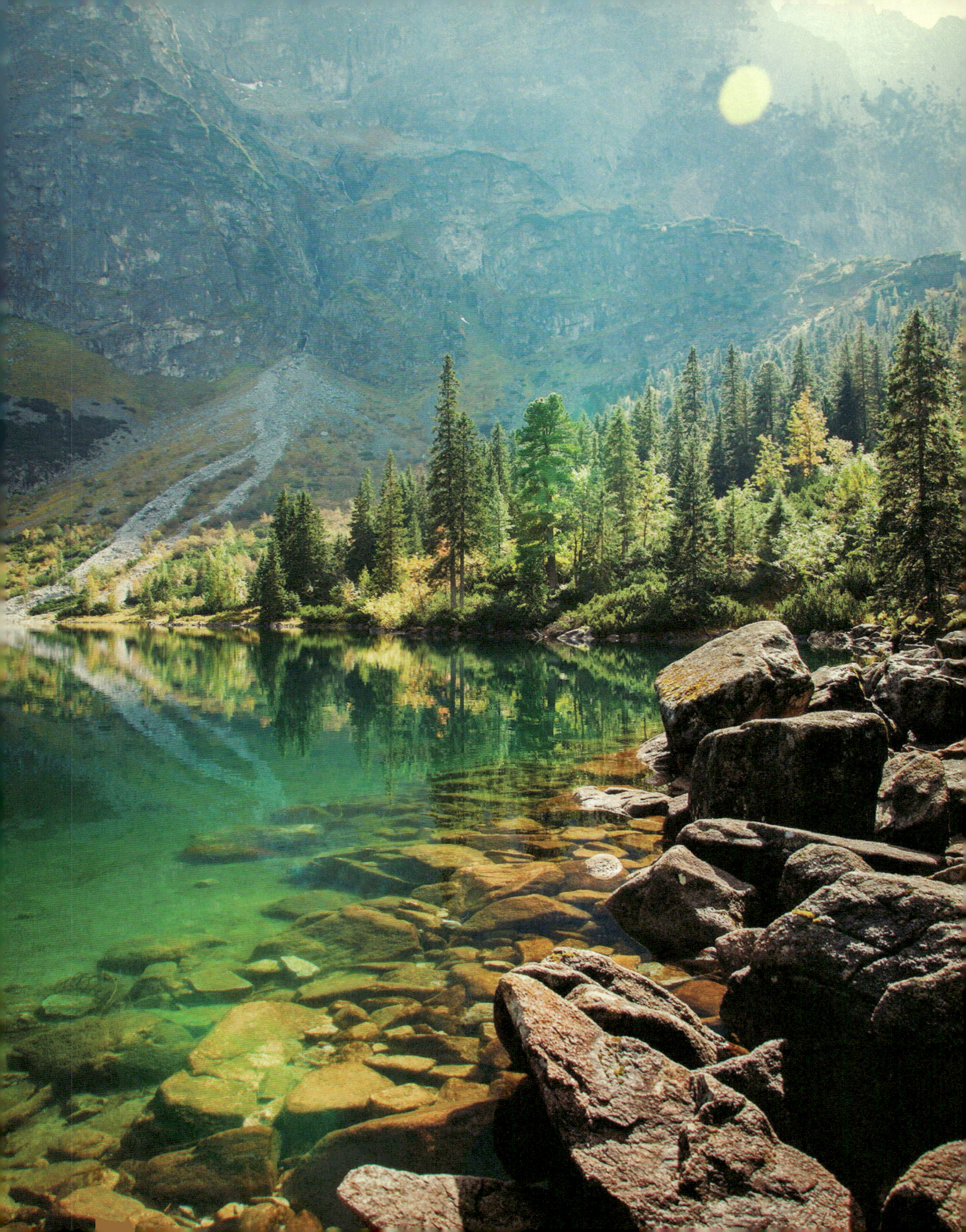

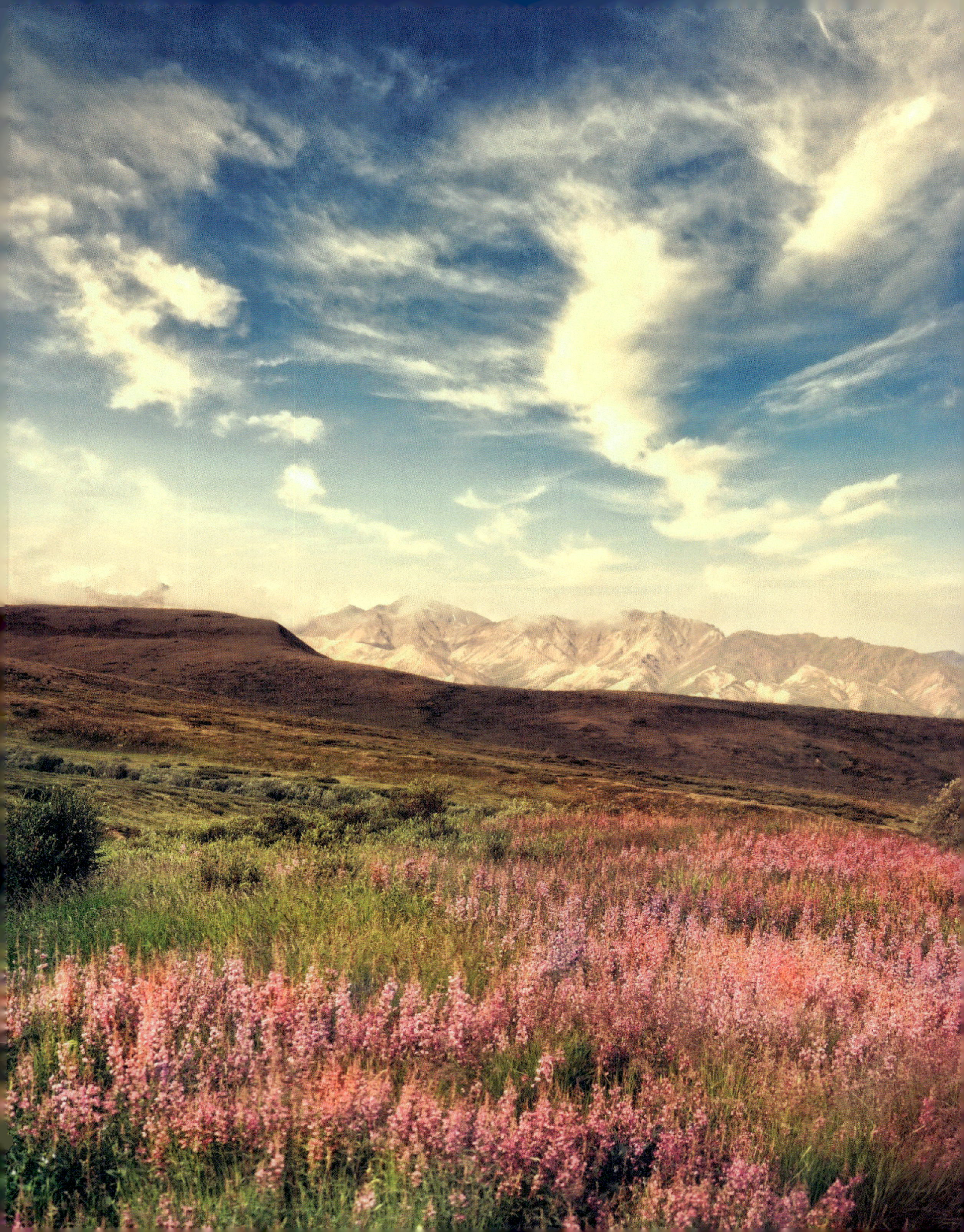

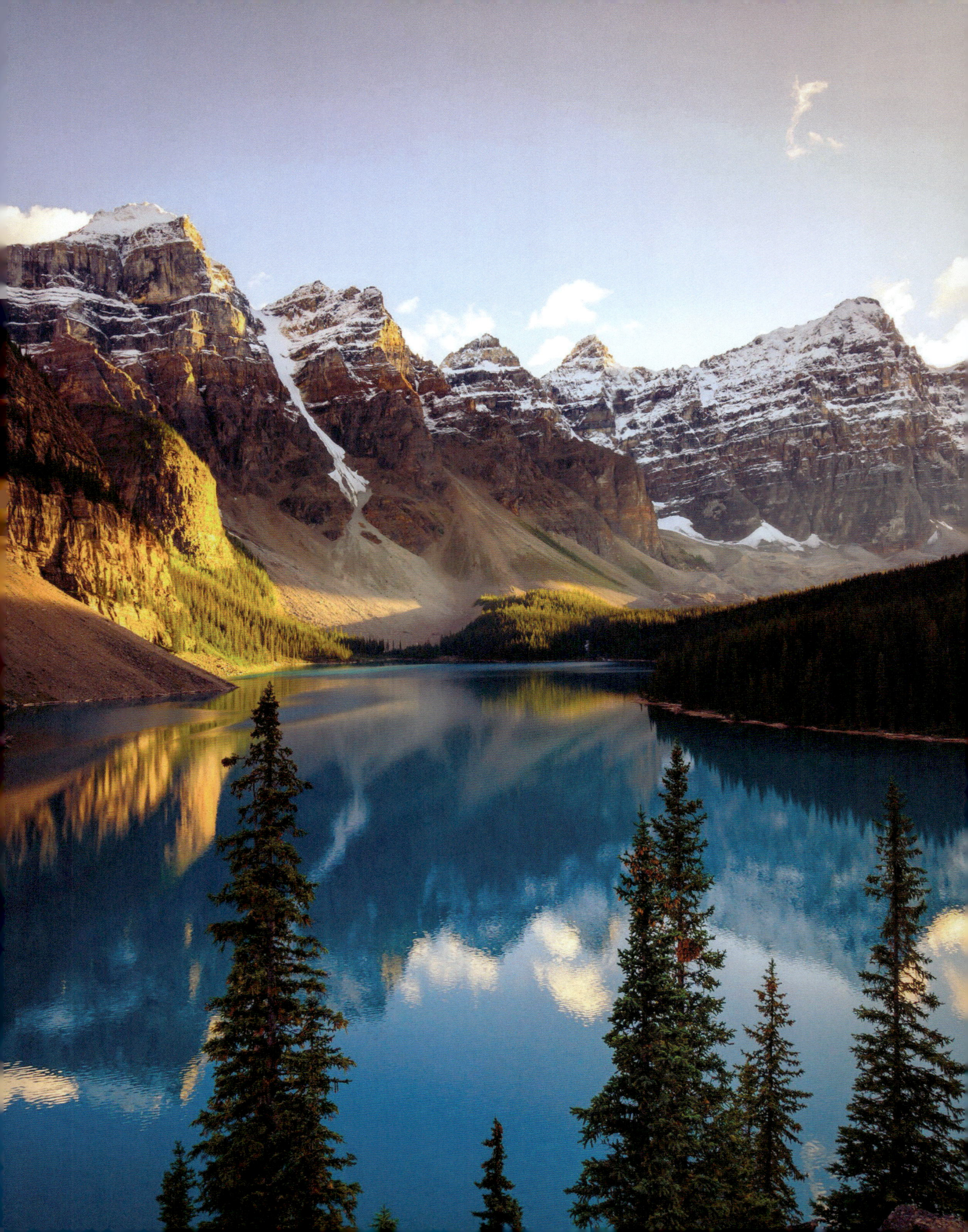

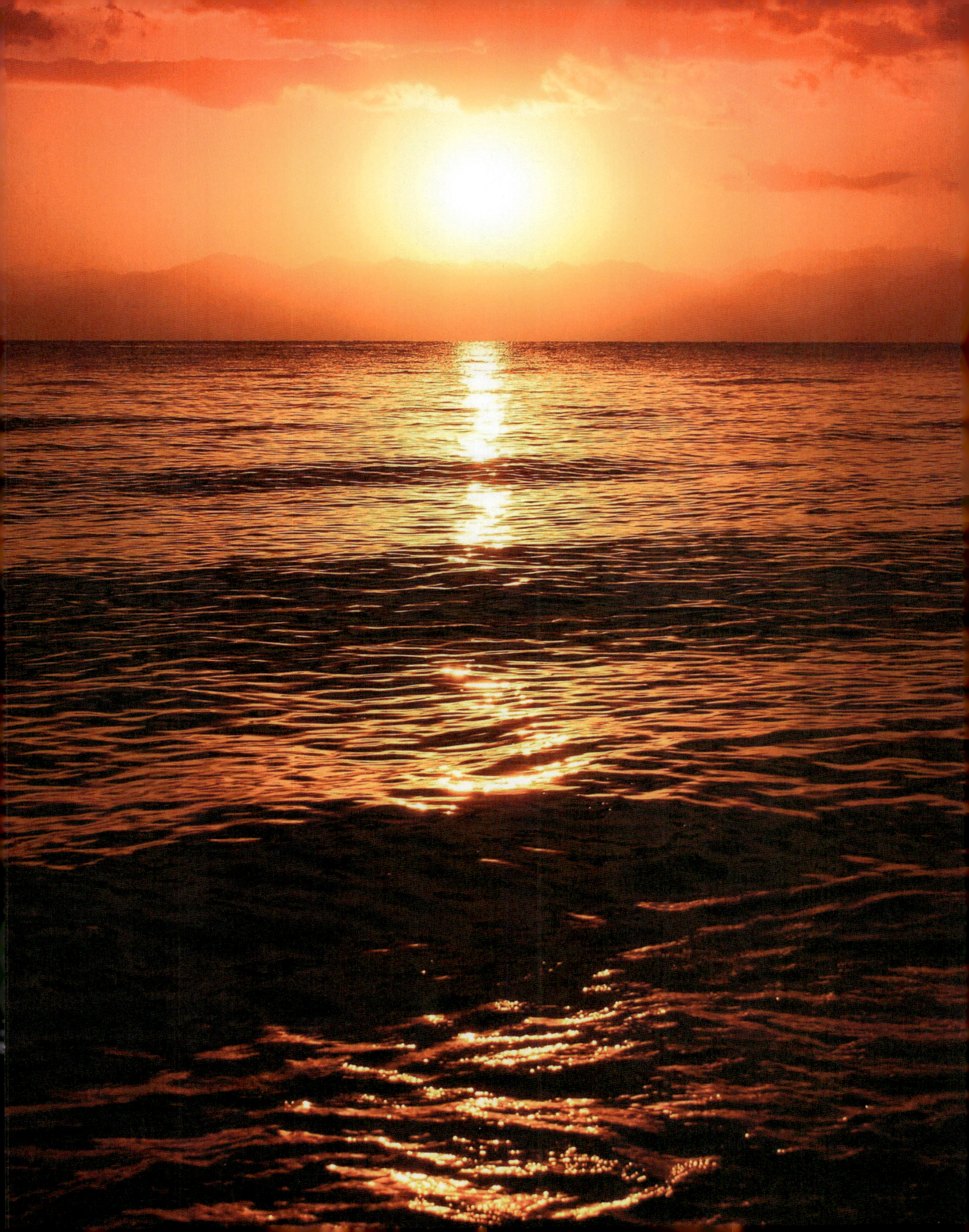

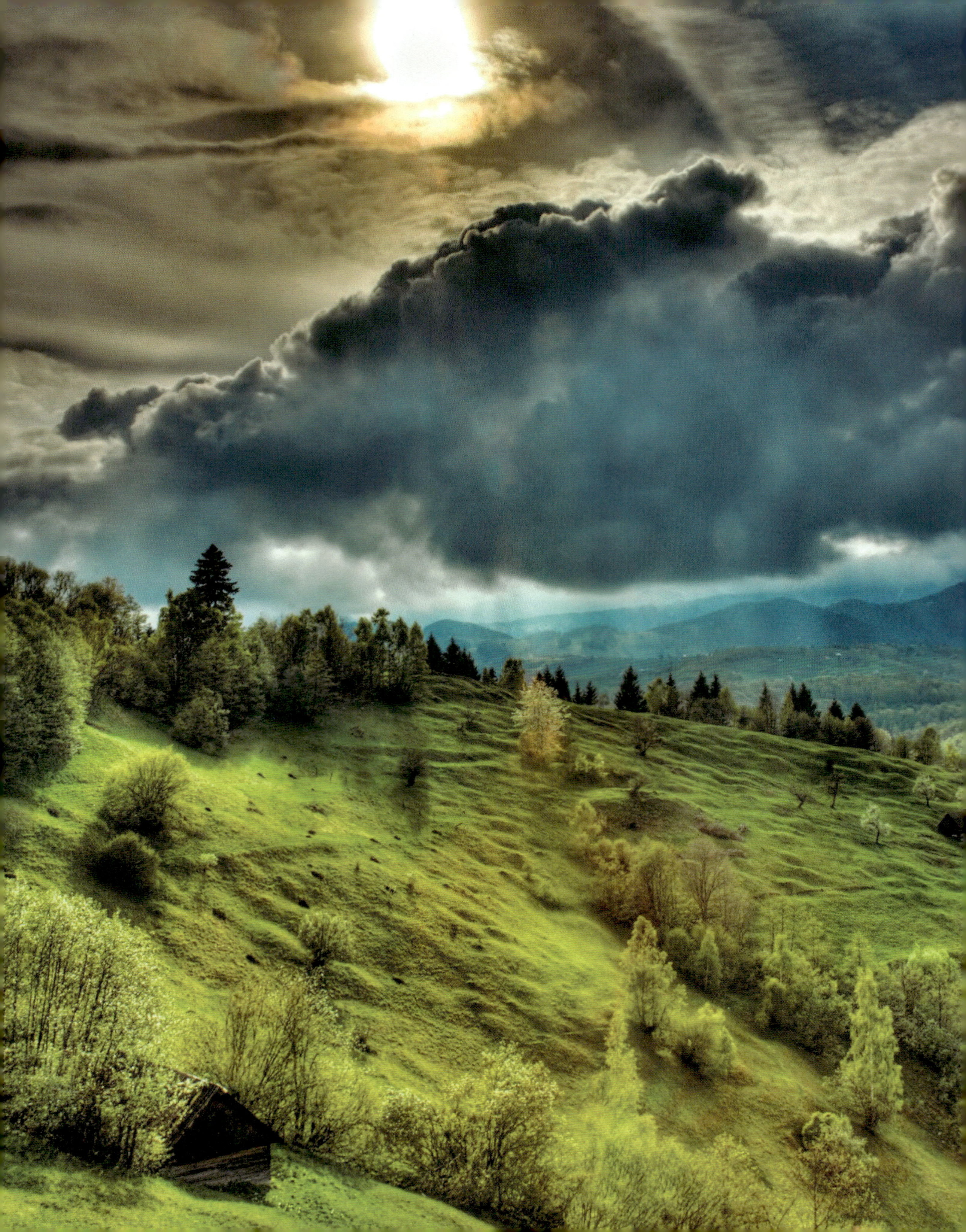

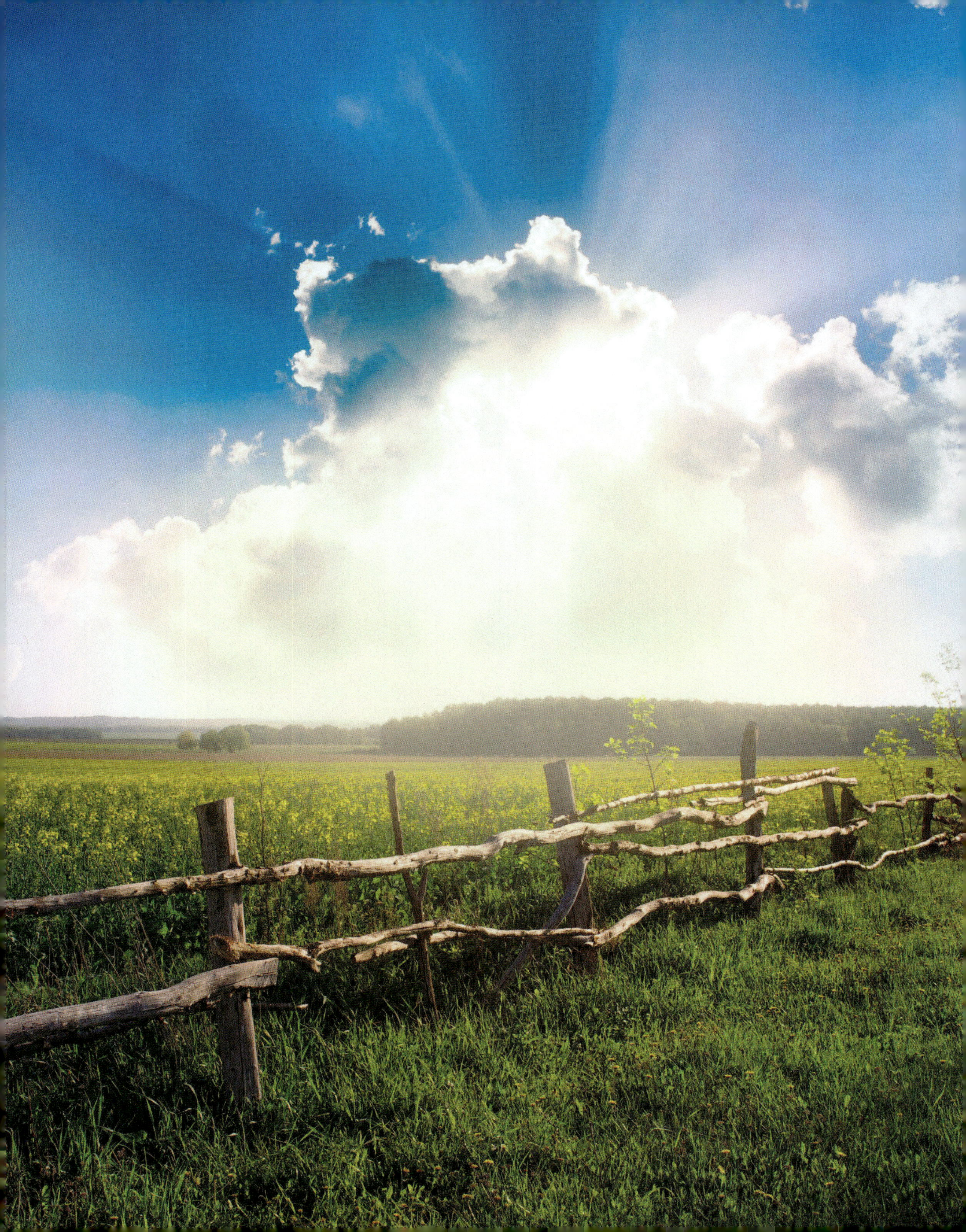

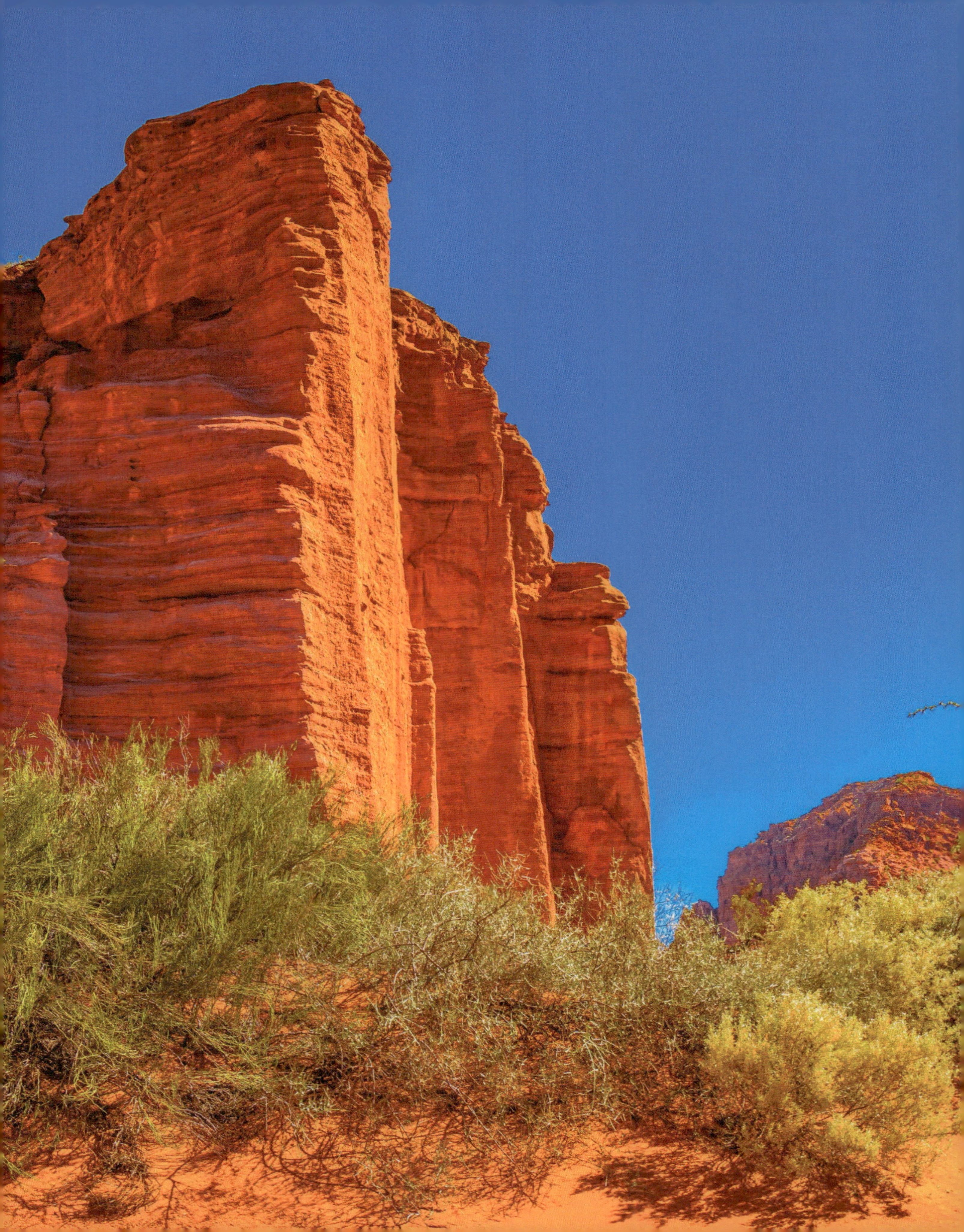

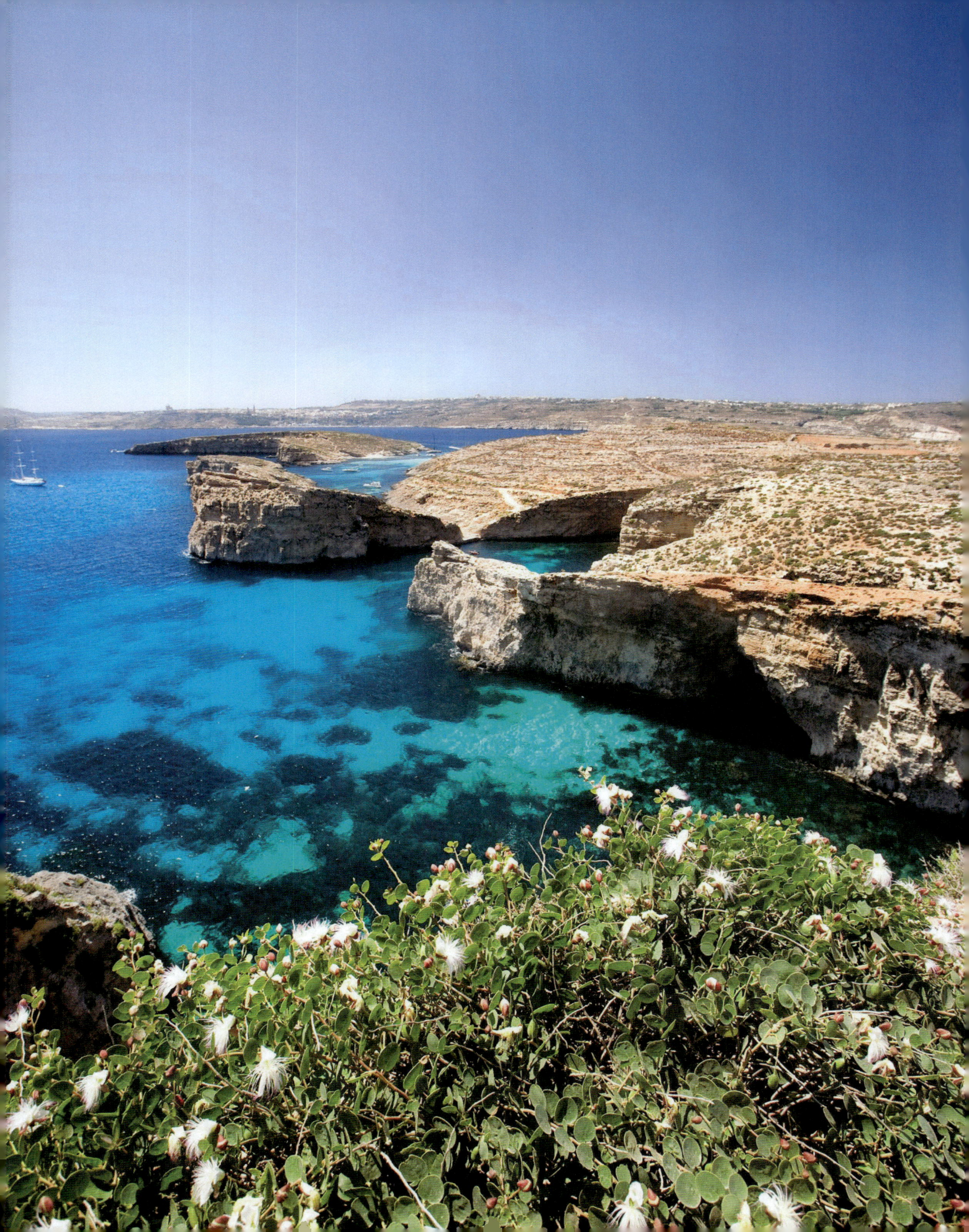

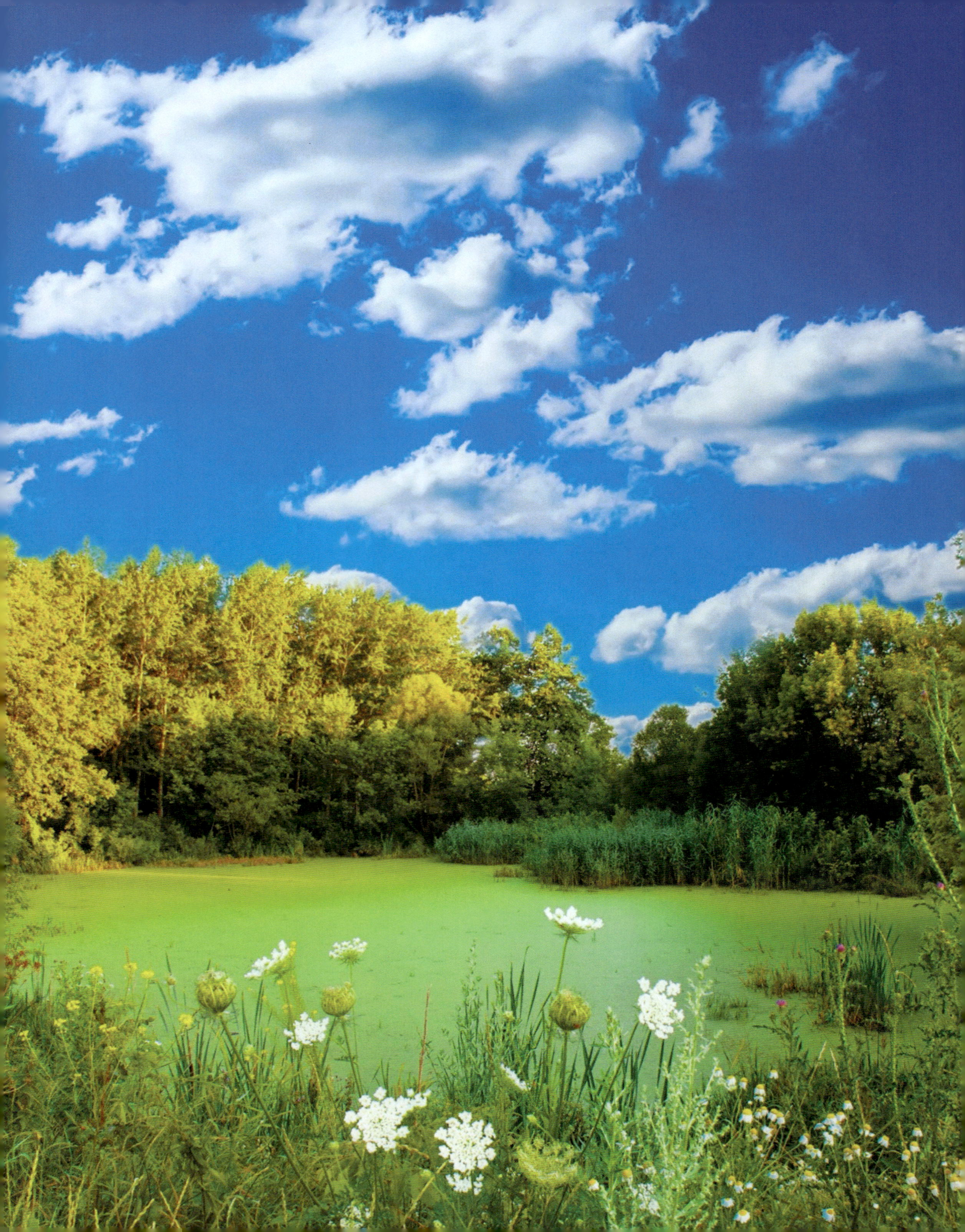

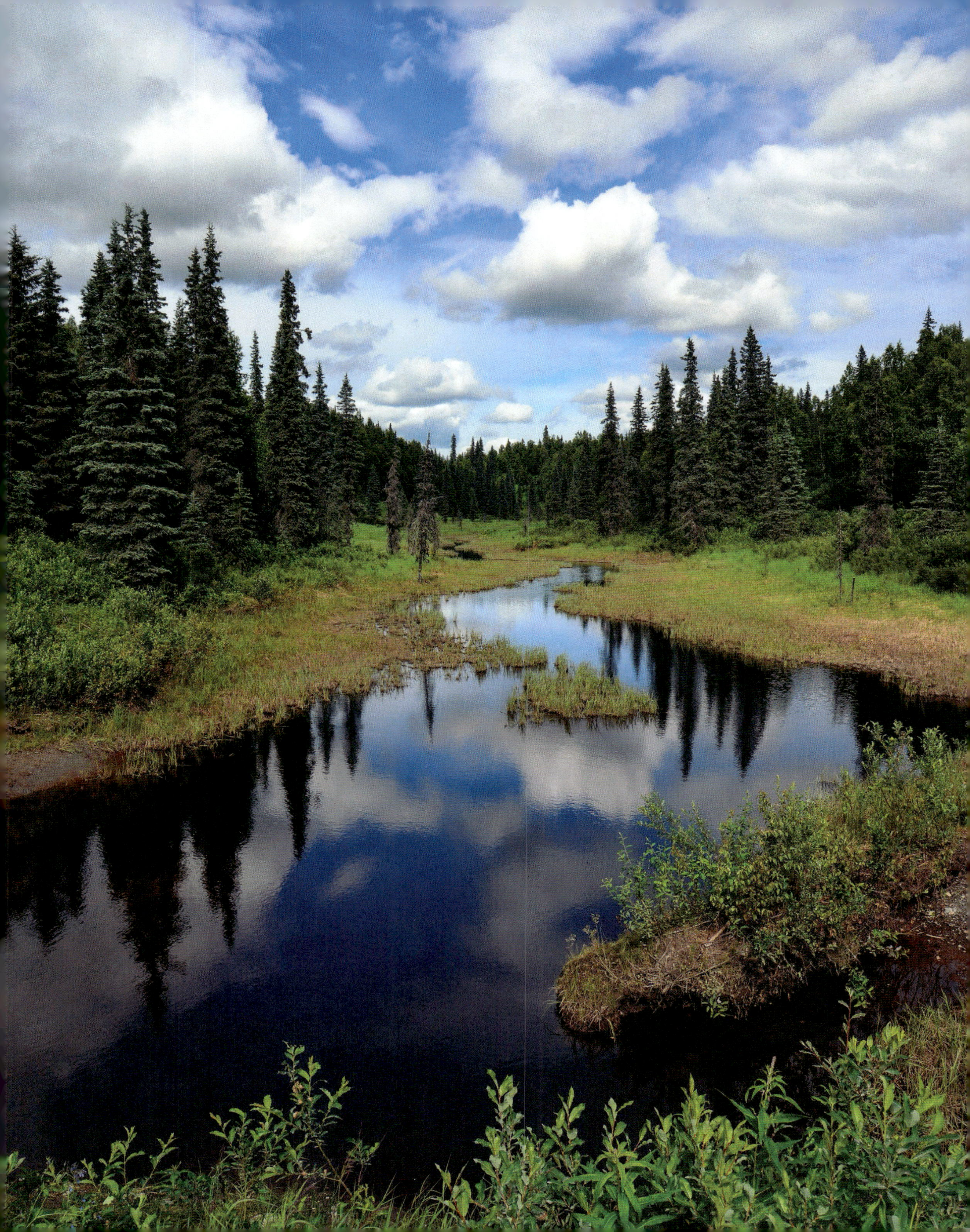

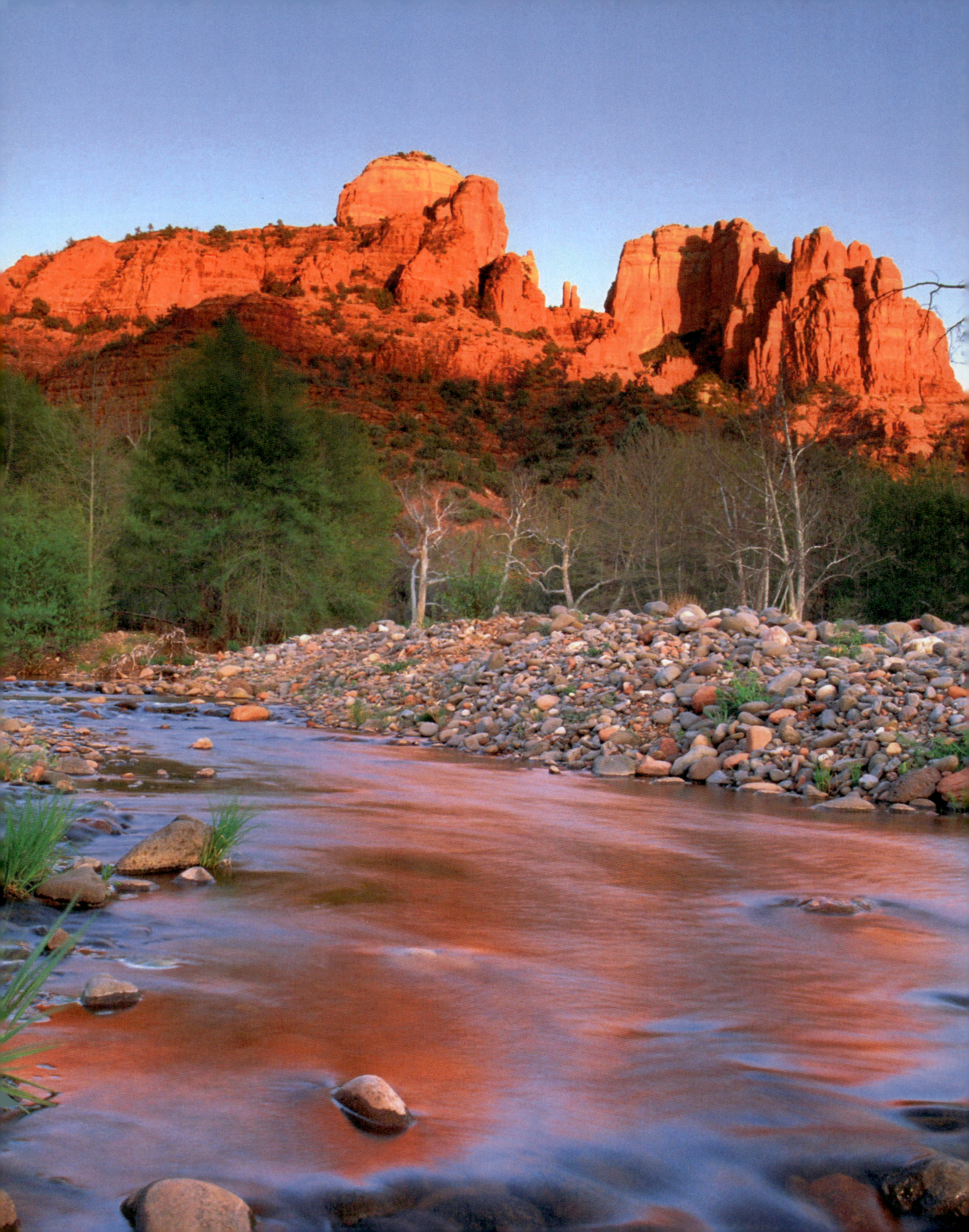

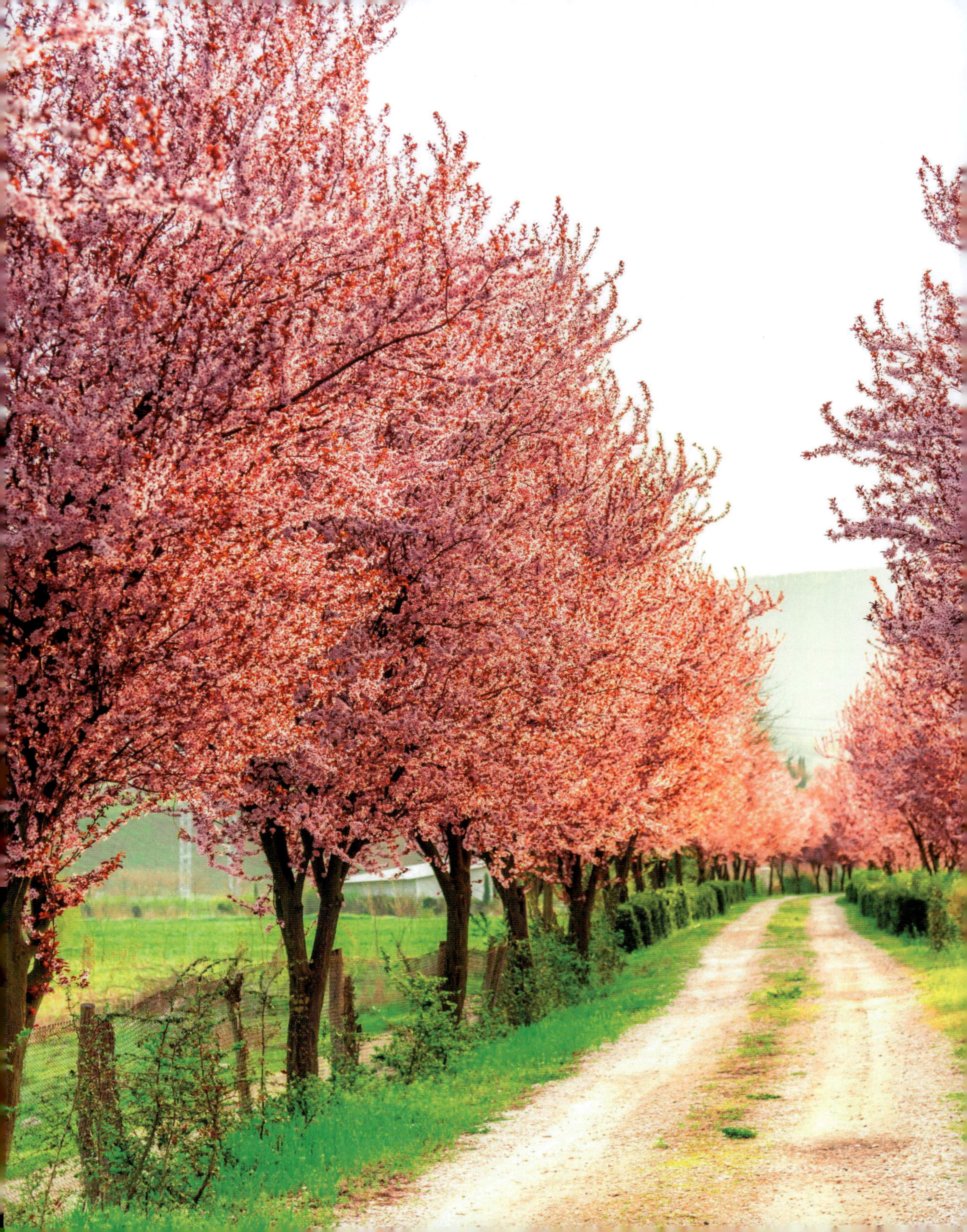

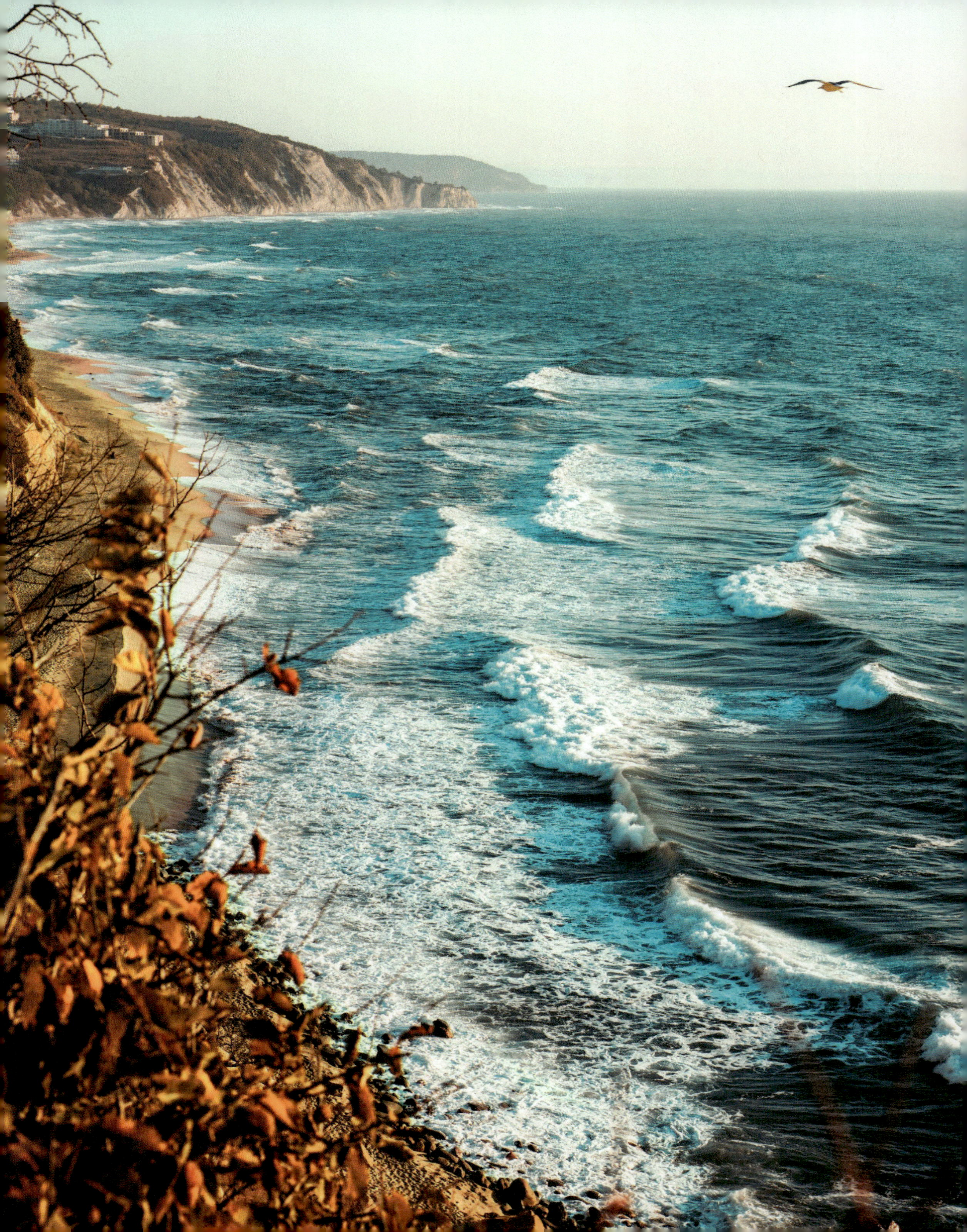

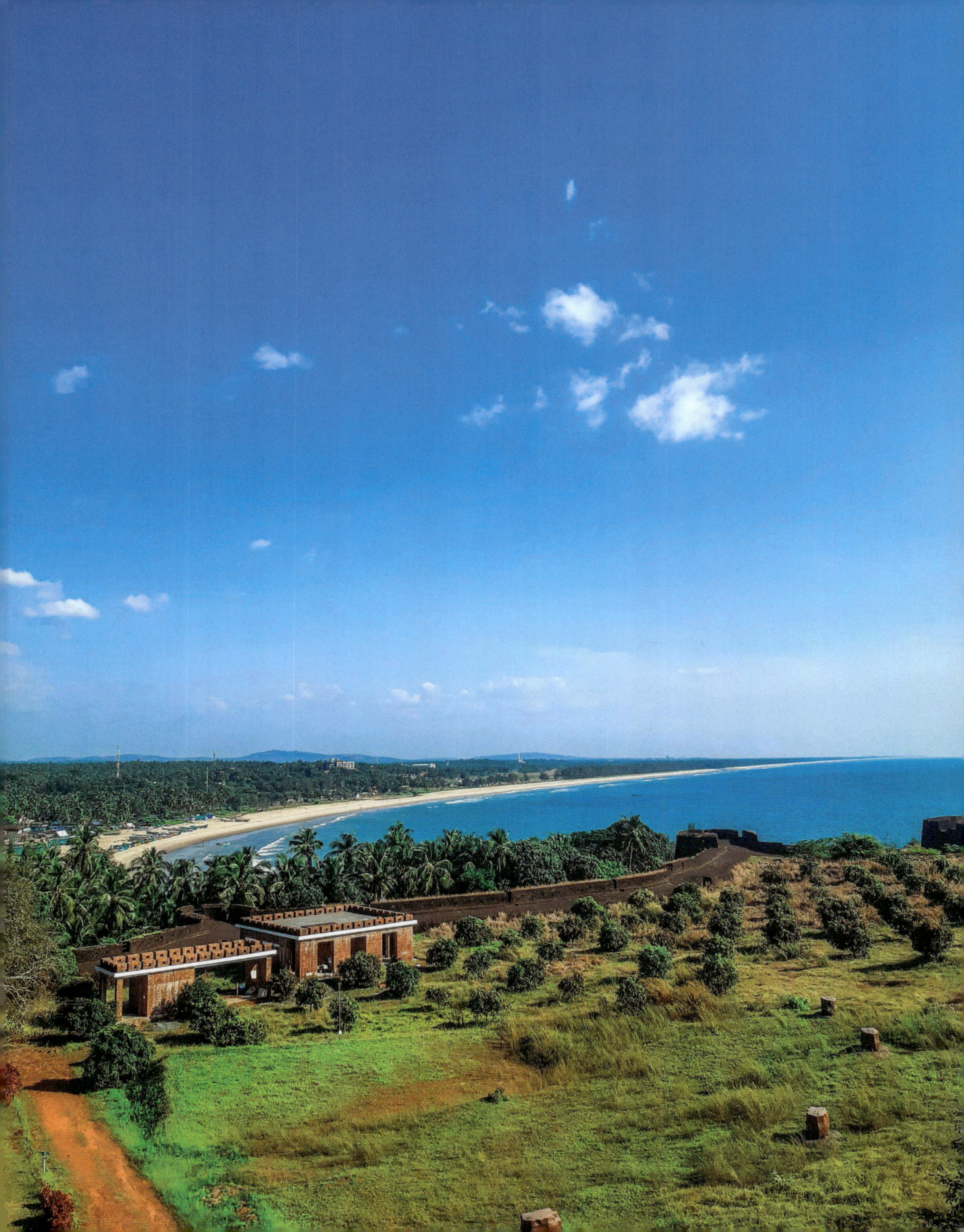

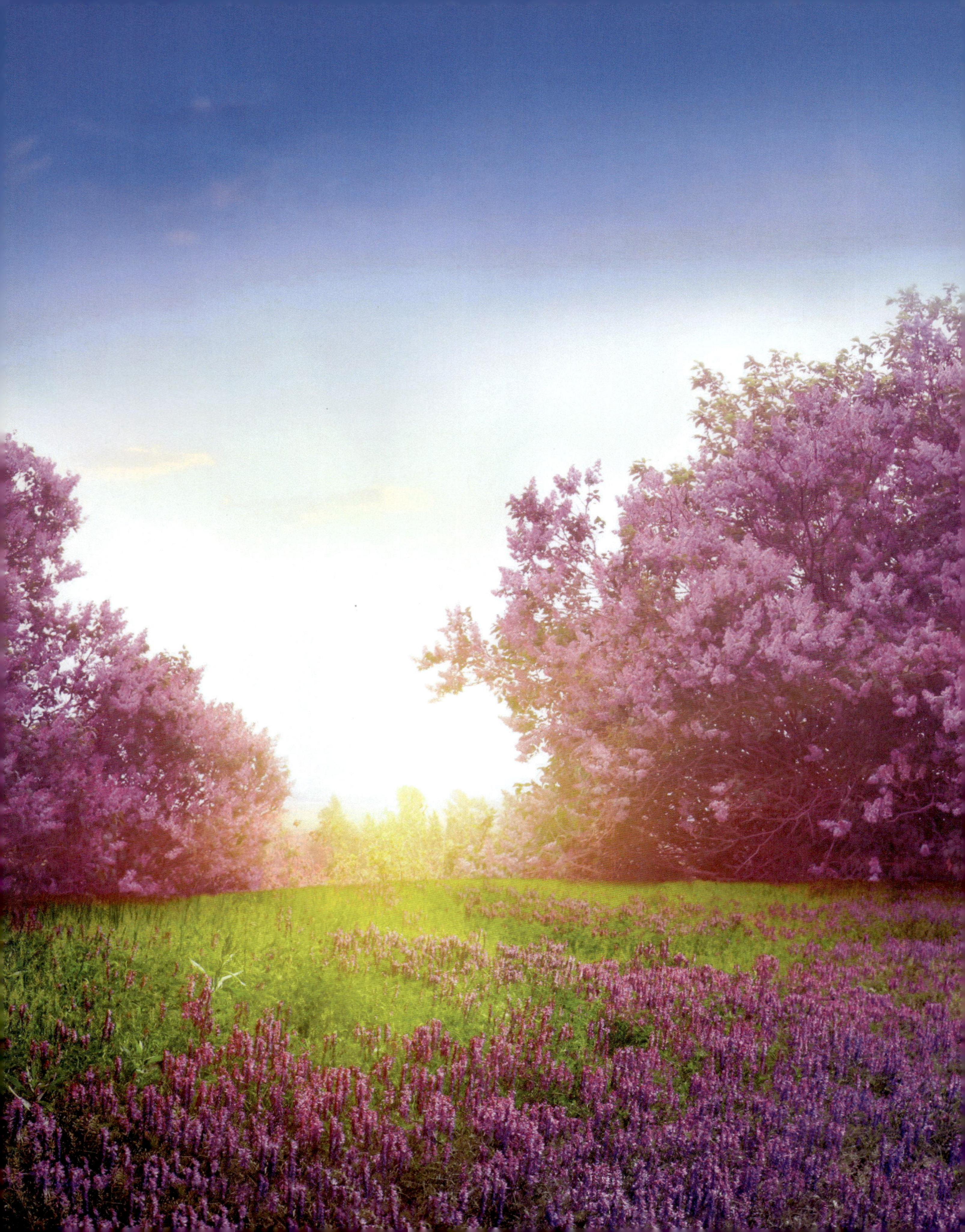

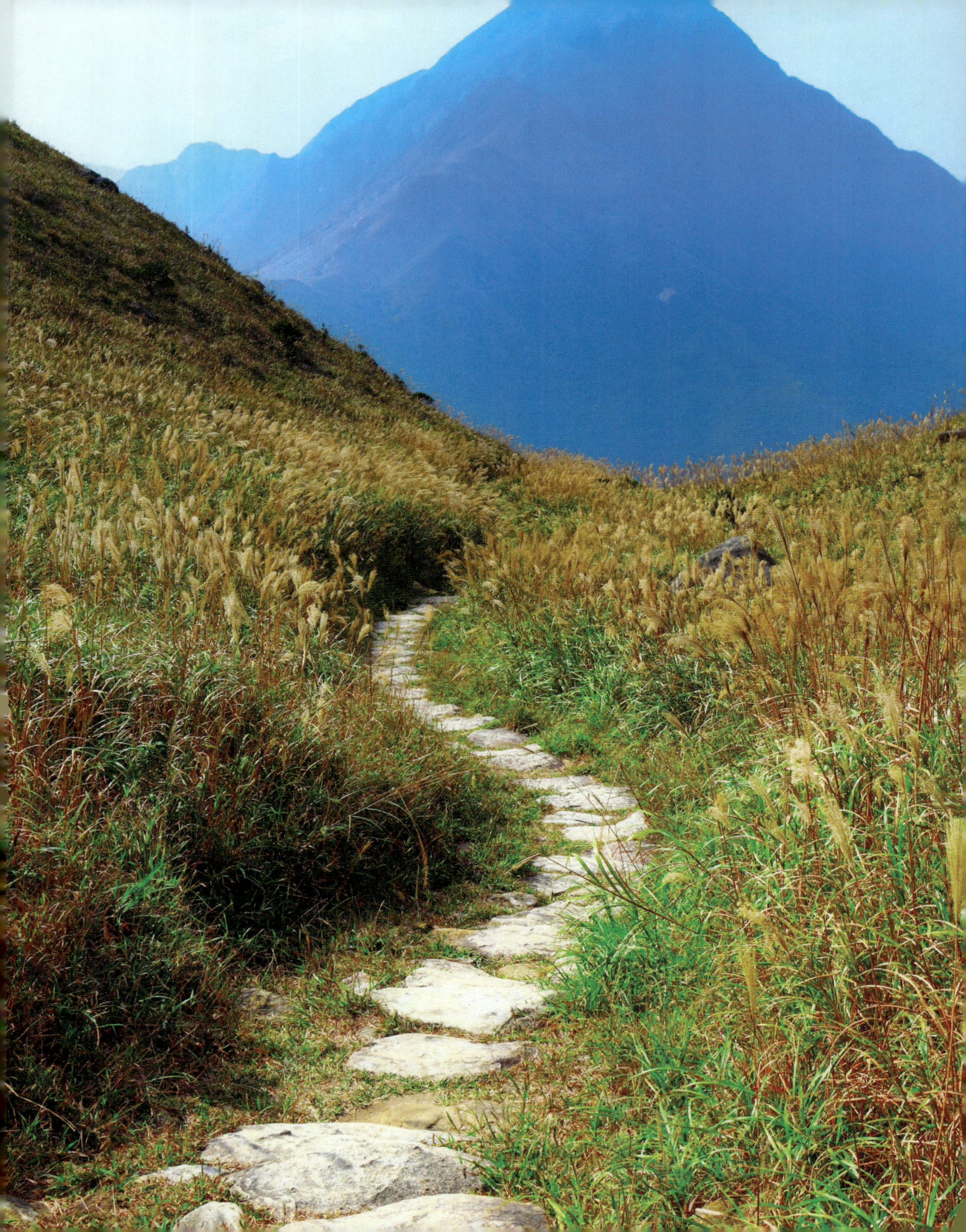

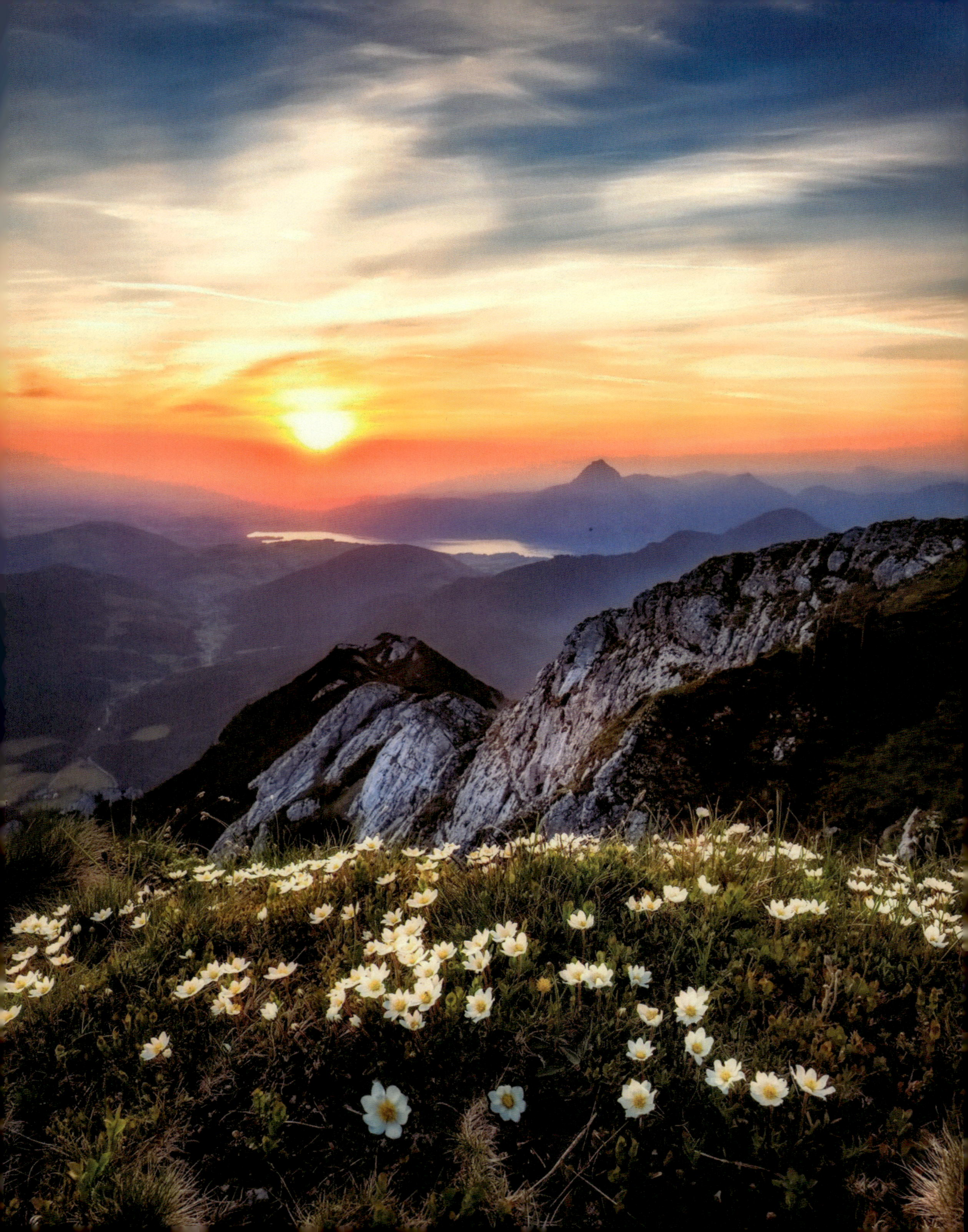

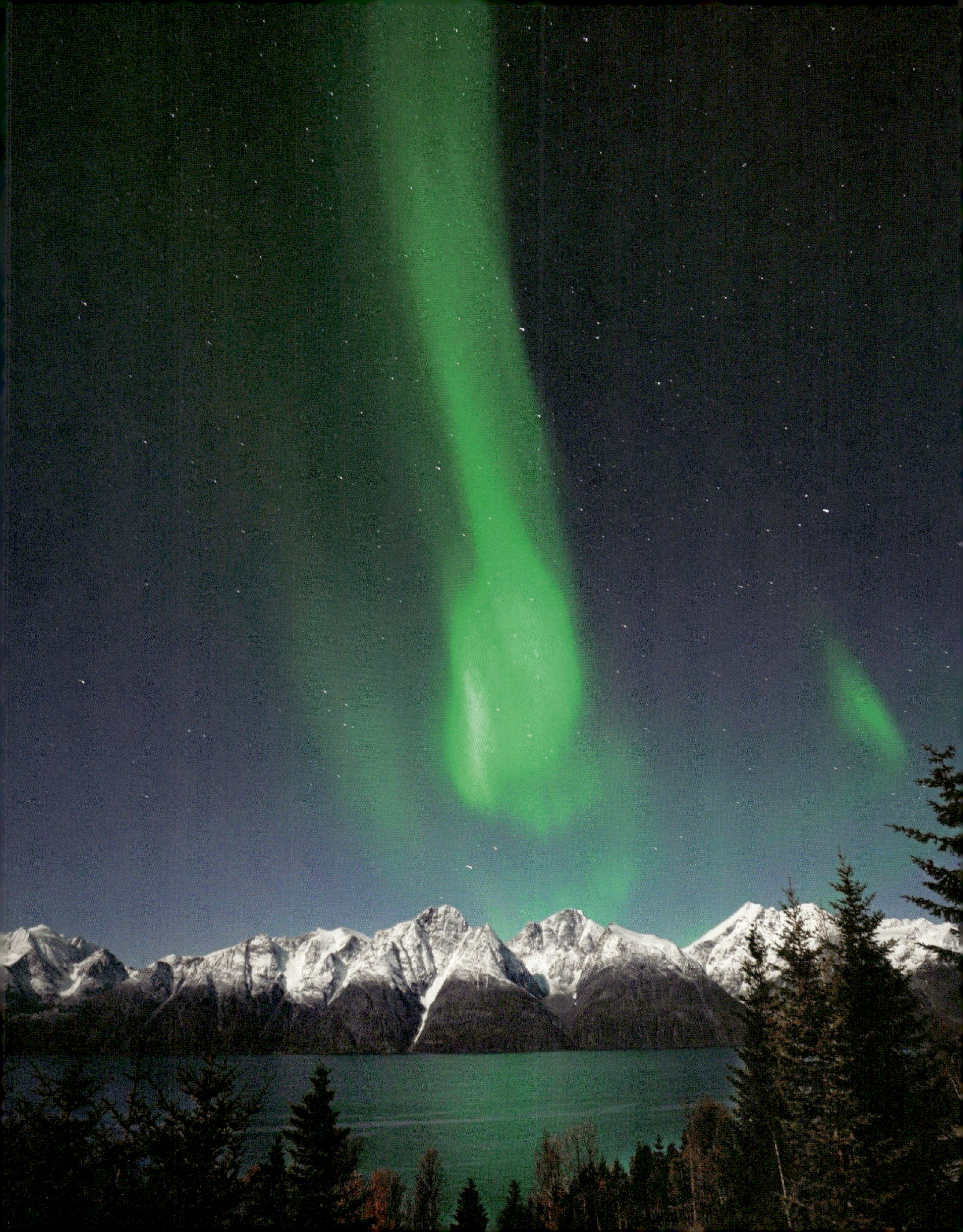

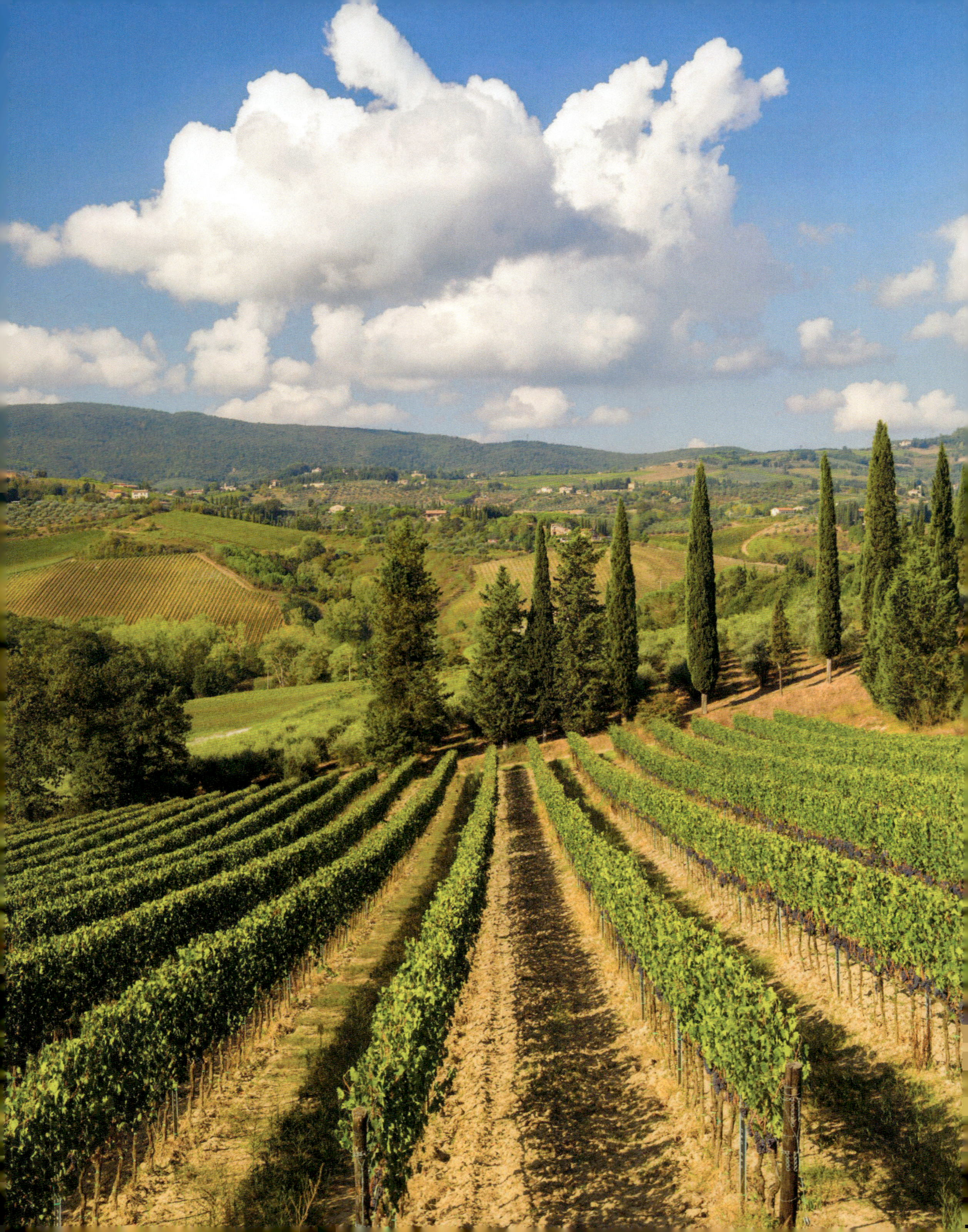

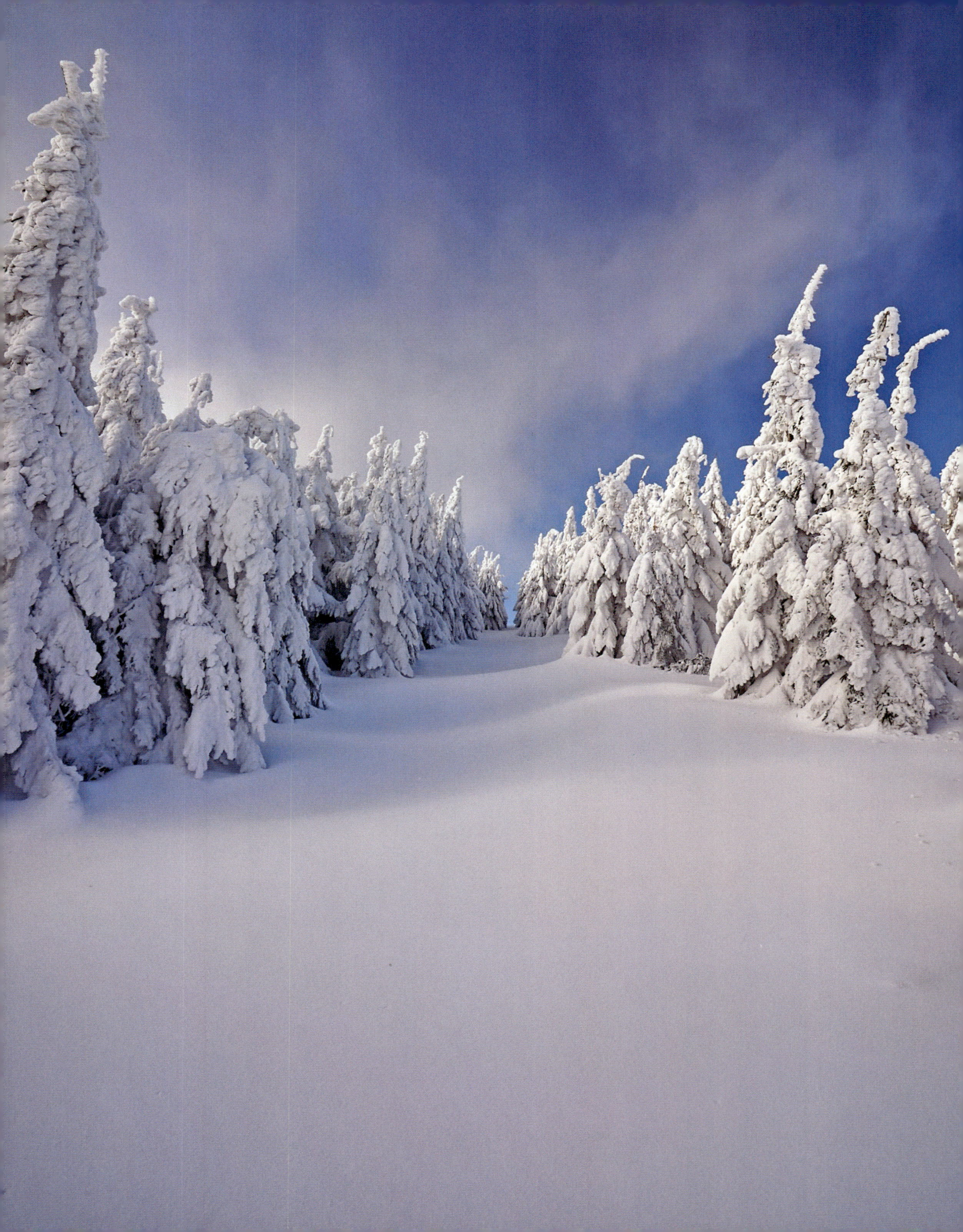

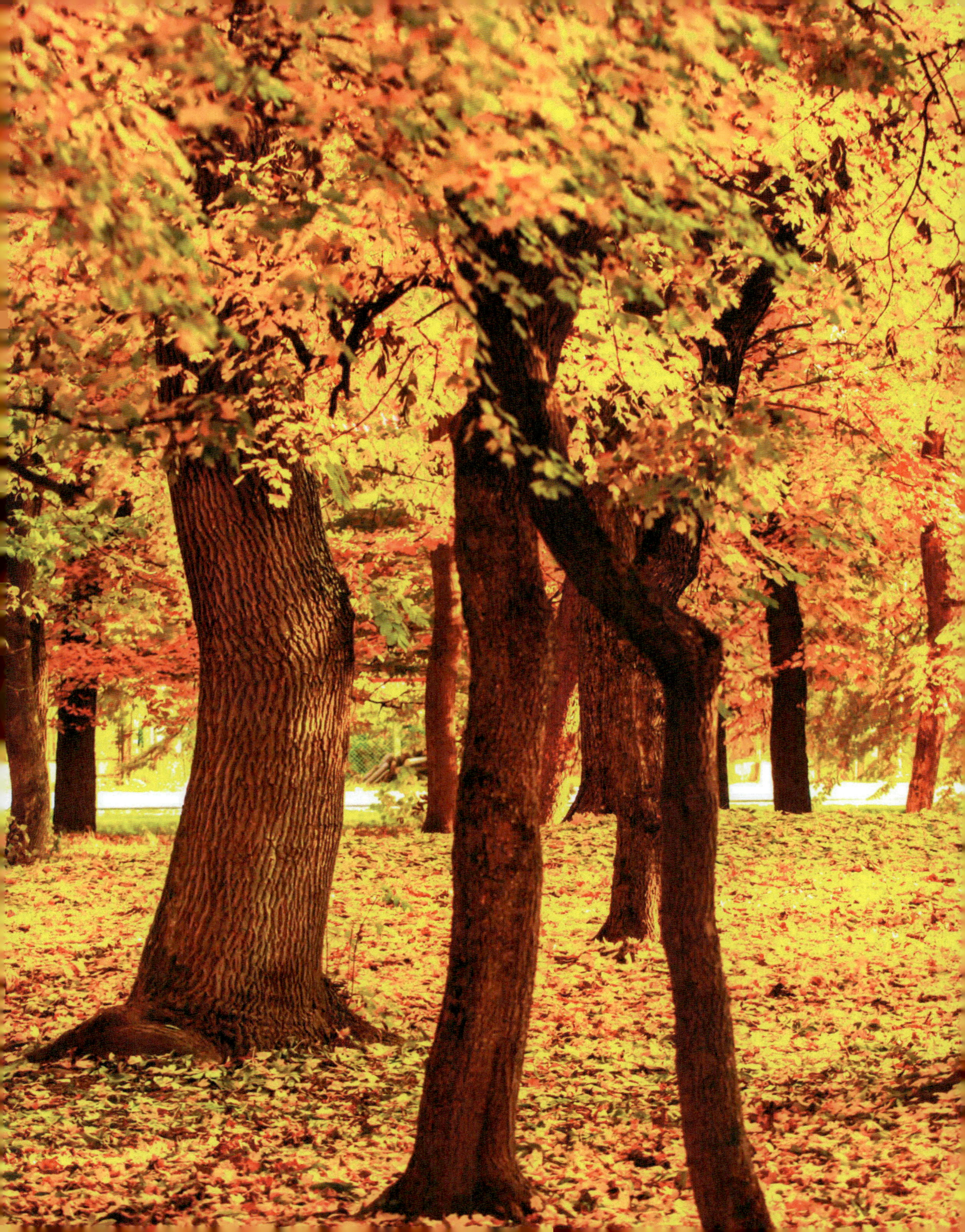

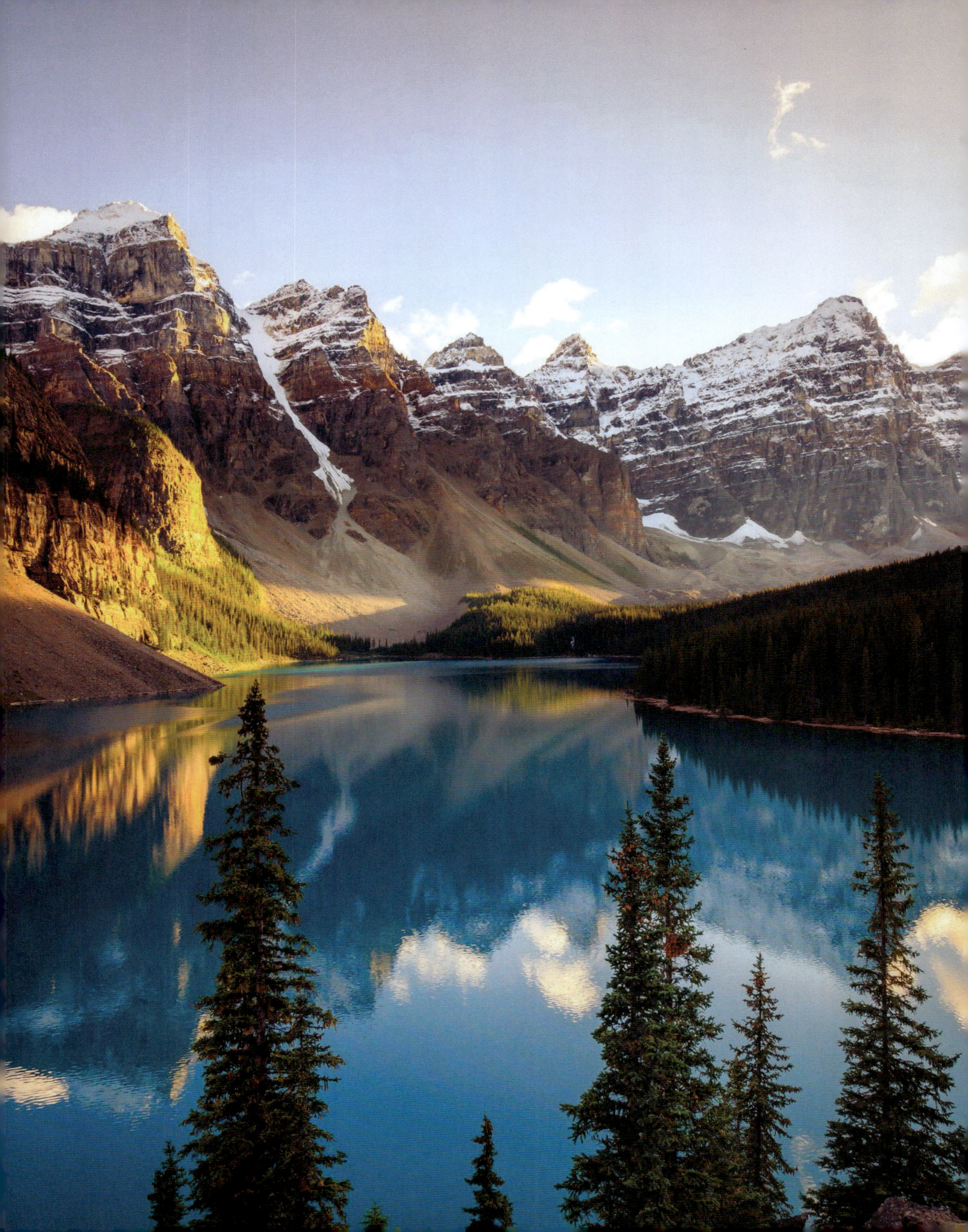

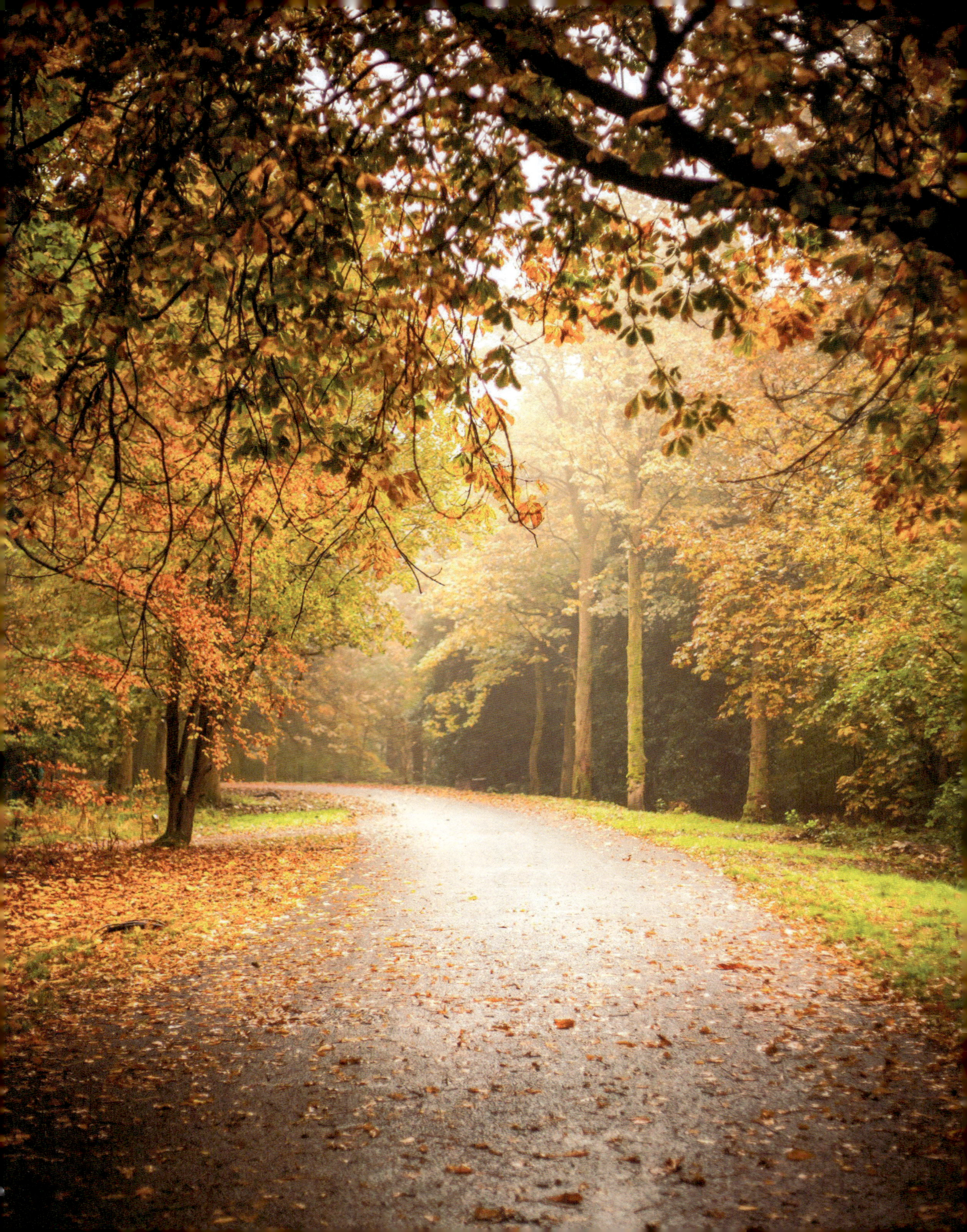

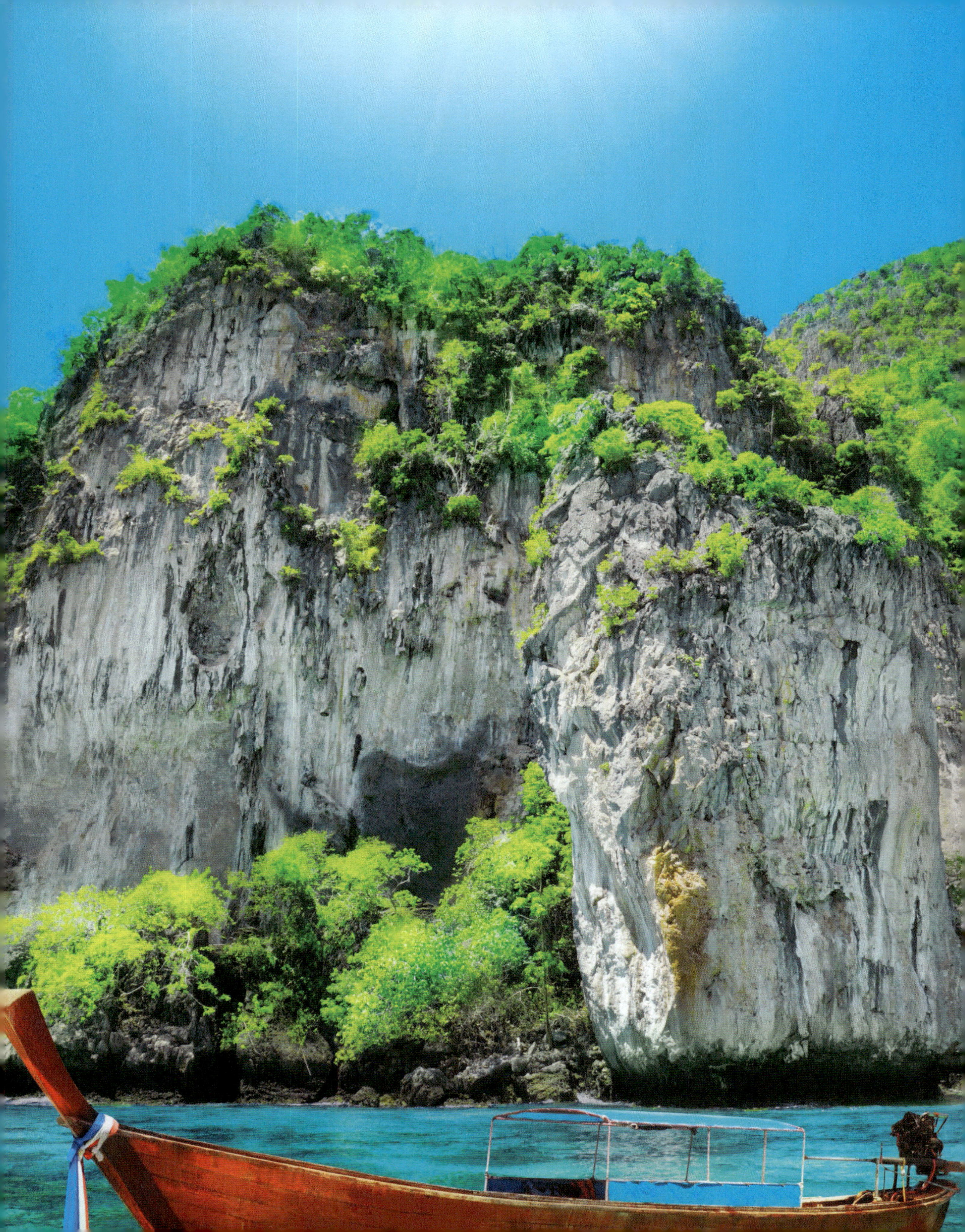

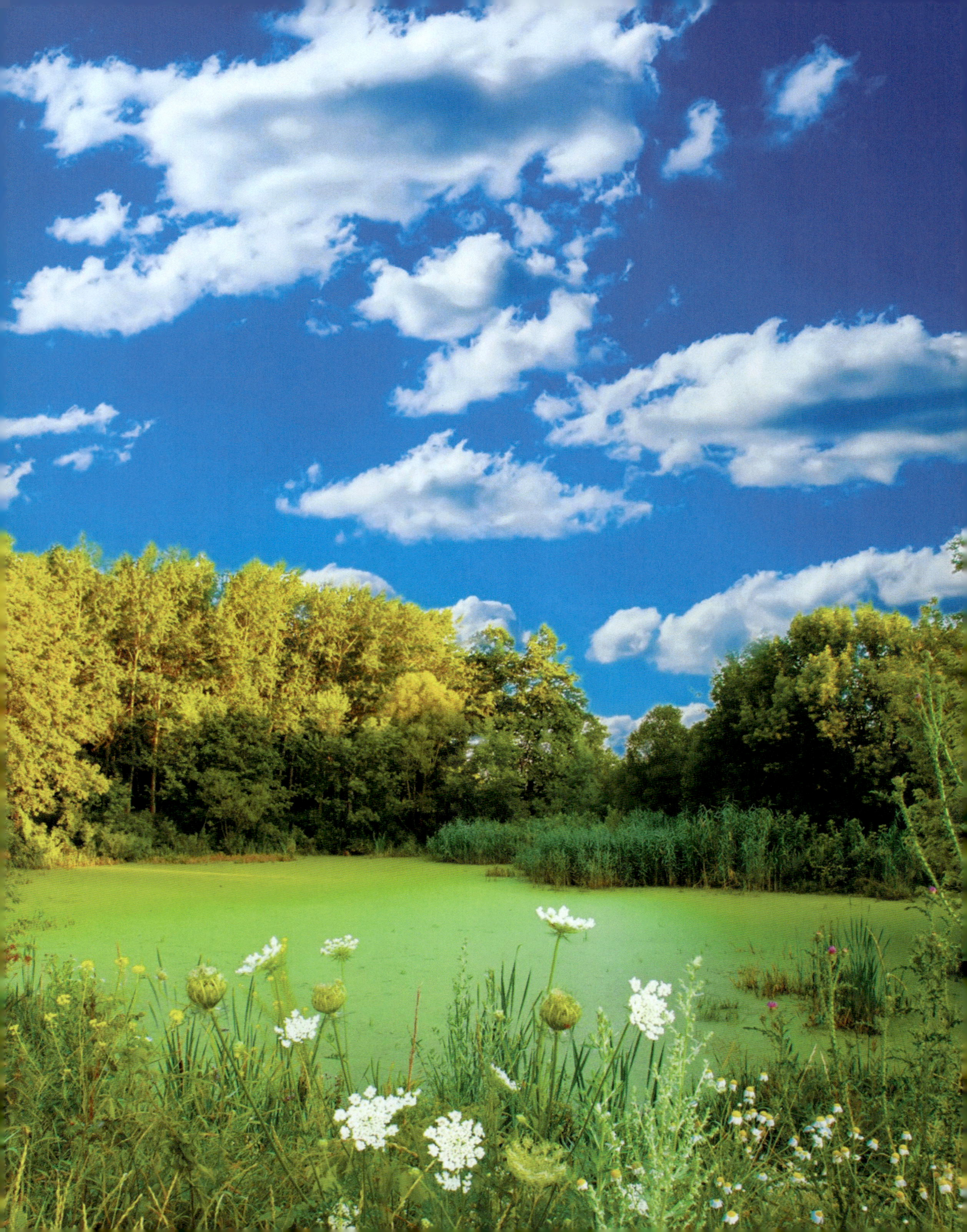

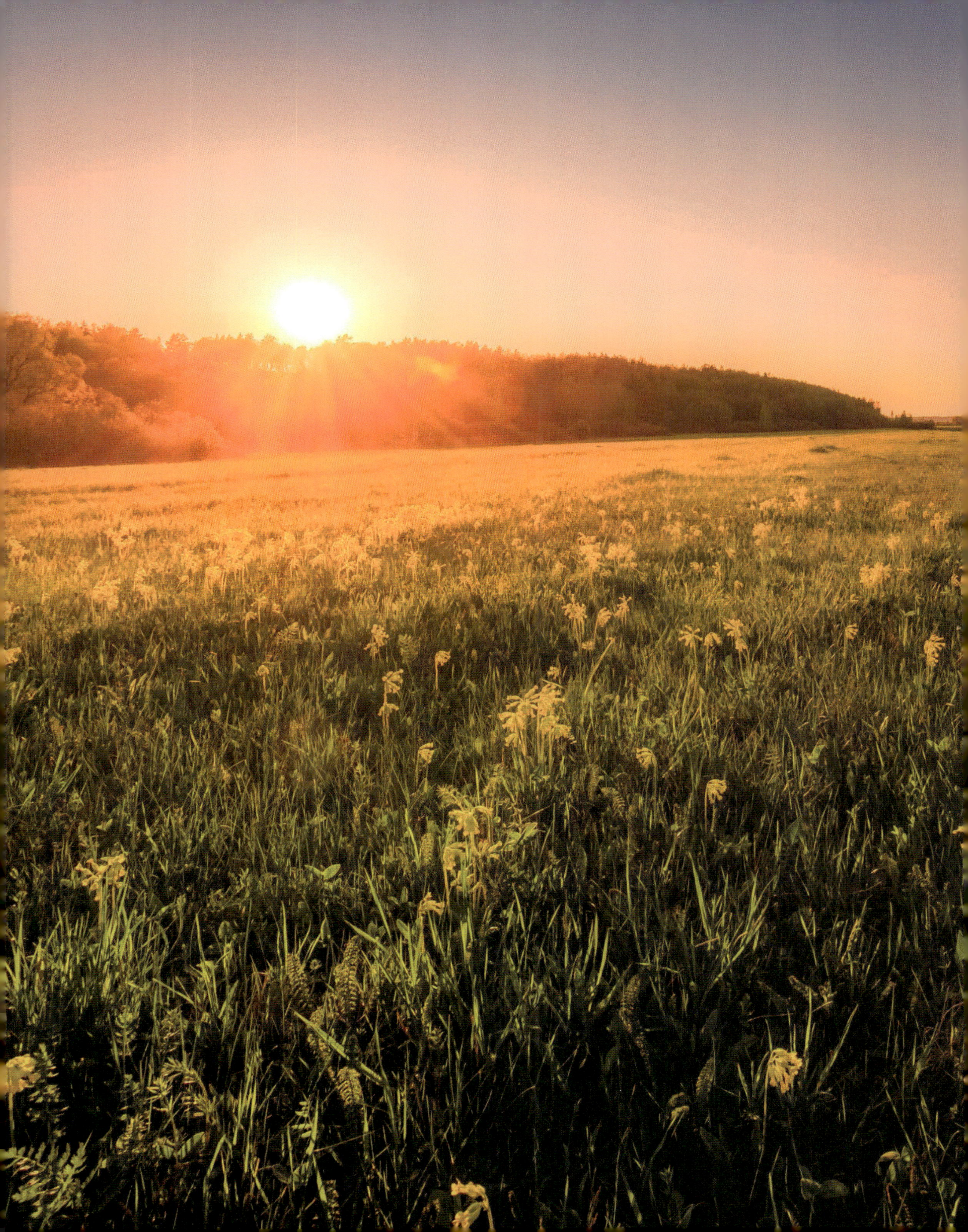

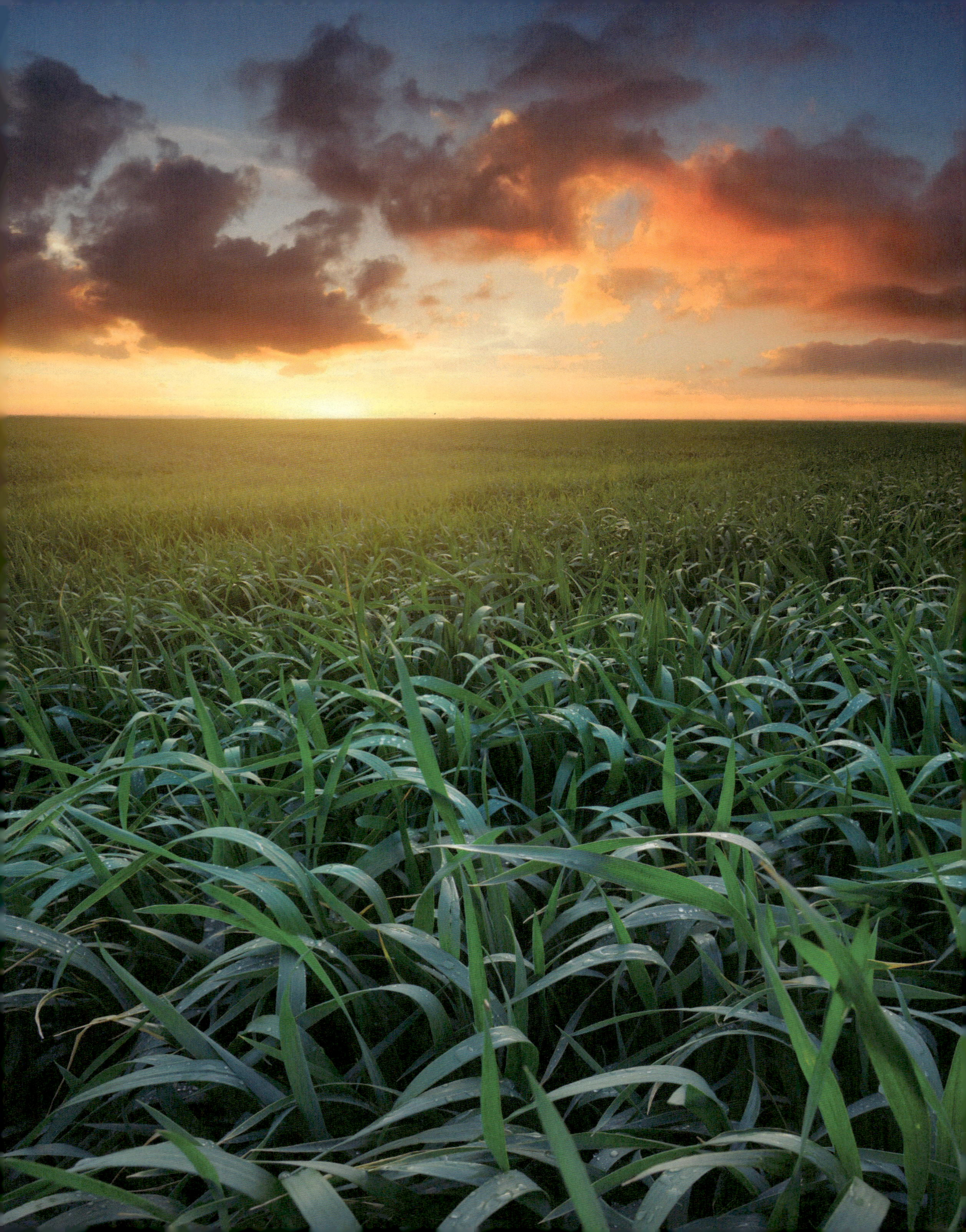

Printed in Great Britain
by Amazon

37644039R00025